On the Fringes of Europe

By the same author

Memories of Childhood

On the Fringes of Europe

Student Years 1956-1963

Martin Nicholson

© 2011 Martin Nicholson

All Rights Reserved

ISBN 978-1-4709-8132-7

2nd Edition

For Raili

CONTENTS

Preface

One

National Service 1956-1958: Something Special *11*

Two

Spanish Interlude: Travels with a Donkey *45*

Three

Cambridge 1958-1961:
Following in the Family's Footsteps *67*

Four

Moscow University 1961:
Enjoying the Thaw *91*

Five

Moscow University 1962:
'Our Boundless Motherland' *141*

Six

Finland 1962-1963: An Affair of the Heart *159*

OUTLINE MAPS
Showing principal places mentioned in the text

Map 1: The British Isles: 187

Map 2: The Iberian Peninsula: 188

Map 3: Finland and the USSR in Europe: 189

Preface

In 2008 I published privately my *Memories of Childhood*, now republished, which took me from birth in 1937, through childhood in South America and England, to the point where I left school in 1955, aged eighteen.

This volume takes the story to 1963, when I was preparing to get married. The title takes some liberties with both space and time. I was hardly on a fringe of Europe when studying Russian in London, though in East Fife I certainly was, while Cambridge felt like the edge of the world when an east wind was blowing across from the Urals. Nor, strictly speaking, was I a student when earning my living as a teacher in Finland. But my frame of mind was still that of a student: I took things as they came without much of a thought as to where they were leading.

As with the earlier volume I owe a great deal to my son Colin for his efforts to dig below the surface of memory. I am also grateful to fellow students of former years, in particular Roger Bartlett, Godfrey Garrett and Brian Murphy for their comments and suggestions. But only I can be held responsible for the content.

Martin Nicholson

September 2011

One

National Service 1956-1958: Something Special

Bring back National Service!

For decades now, crusty old gentlemen have been calling for the reintroduction of National Service as a way to instil discipline into the feckless youth of the day. They are barking up the wrong tree. Peacetime National Service was a continuation of the conscription laws that had been in force during the Second World War. It was not designed to give idle youths a sense of purpose, but to maintain the country's armed forces at a high level as the clouds of the Cold War gathered. No sooner had the war against Germany been won than a new threat from Communist Russia and its satellites was upon us. Originally set at one and a half years, the period of service was extended to two years at the onset of the Korean War in 1950. National Service was phased out only in 1960, so those like me, born in 1937, knew that we would have to go through it when we were eighteen.

It did have the reputation of being a tough couple of years, and at school we eagerly quizzed returning old boys about their experiences in the Armed Forces. It was my good fortune to hear from one of them that rather than 'square bashing' (drilling) or scrubbing the decks you could spend your time in the Forces learning Russian. This was an appealing idea. Languages were my forte, and together with a school friend I had already made a start on Russian. I also knew that the Royal Navy, unlike the other Services, pre-selected their candidates for the Russian courses. So I made sure I could get into the Navy by joining the Royal Naval Volunteer Reserve (RNVR) from school. By the time I left school at the end of 1955 I had already done a fortnight's initial training on the aircraft carrier HMS *Theseus*, safely tied up in Portland harbour. I had my naval kit in my kitbag and was ready to go.

I knew I would be called up in the next six months, but I didn't know when. So I decided to get a job. I went to Gabbitas Thring, the well-known educational consultants, to offer my services as a teacher. They quickly found out that King's House School in Richmond, a private boys' day school conveniently close to home, was looking for someone to teach English and History. Within days the kindly and open-hearted headmaster, Mr Pattullo, had taken me on. He fully realised that I had few qualifications for these two subjects, having offered French and Spanish, but the spring term had already started, and he was desperately short staffed. Just eighteen and a half myself, I had no idea how to manage a class of ten-year old boys and felt I had nothing to impart to them beyond what was in the text book. My only release was afternoon sports, where I coached them in rugby, but in reality played out my fantasies of being a real player myself, effortlessly eluding the clutches of creatures half my size. Many years later I was to see an embarrassingly similar scene played out by the schoolmaster in Ken Loach's film *Kes* – evidently I was not the only one to have had such fantasies.

After only a month of teaching I got my call-up papers and said good-bye to King's House School without regret. By happy coincidence, I had been teaching alongside a young Russian émigré, Sergei Hackell. He went on to become a Russian Orthodox priest and well-known broadcaster on the BBC Russian Service, and his mother taught at one of the Russian courses for National Servicemen that I was to join. He was the first Russian I had ever met. Small, bearded and lively, he was popular among the boys and imbued me with a delicious sense of anticipation. So it was a cheerful and slightly cocky young man, kitbag over his shoulder, who reported to Victoria Barracks, Portsmouth, on 5th March 1956 as a Probationary Coder (Special).

We 'Specials' were a group of a dozen or more young men who had been selected to join the stream of would-be Russian linguists and were easily distinguished in the barracks by our studious and middle class appearance. We were bound for university; a couple had already graduated. Happily, the other group of National Servicemen with whom we shared our large mess were also a cut above the educational norm: they were artificers, men who had learnt a trade and had been called up only after they had finished their apprenticeship so that the Navy could use their skills. Older than us, a number of them newly married, they tended to sit around discussing intimate details of their sex life in a fascinating but embarrassing way. They teased us egg-heads, but not maliciously. There were a few uncomfortable moments, nonetheless. We had to declare formally whether or not we were smokers and thus entitled or not entitled to a ration of cheap cigarettes. The artificers exerted none too subtle pressure on the non-smokers among us to make a false declaration, collect our ration and re-sell it to them, which was strictly forbidden. Despite the pressure, I resisted, without any ill consequences. In due course I got to know one or two people outside our own circle – a depressed medical orderly with two suicide attempts behind him, who had signed up for 12 years and was desperately regretting it, and a cook, who sought me out to translate love letters to and from the girlfriend he had met on a port visit to Spain. The content was always the same: protestations of eternal love by both, followed by a plea from him that she should come to England where they would marry, met by a quiet insistence from her that he should first come to Spain, marry and then take her back to England.

The Navy's job was to lick us into shape. For someone used to the collective discipline and spartan lifestyle of an English boarding school this was not much of an imposition, though I did object to having my already uncomfortably tight serge suit further trimmed at the waist by the barracks tailor. We Coders were just ordinary 'ratings', as the lower ranks are called, but like other administrative personnel we wore 'fore-and-aft' (i.e. collar and tie) uniforms rather than the traditional bell-bottoms that distinguished real seamen, and once the tailor had done his work on mine, I could only stand rigidly to attention. But that, after all, was the idea, and for everyday wear we had comfortable 'No 8s' made out of good quality cotton. They stood me in good stead as leisure wear well into my married life, to the horror of my children.

A week after joining up I took the third and hardest swimming test of my life – three lengths of the pool dressed in a canvas imitation sailor's suit, with boots. The first length was easy – the air trapped inside the canvas gave me buoyancy, but it became a struggle once water penetrated the canvas. With the test behind us we were put to rowing heavy cutters and whalers in the choppy waters of Portsmouth harbour. But we spent much of our time in classrooms learning rules and regulations, basic and not-so-basic hygiene (e.g. sensible precautions when your ship docks at an exotic location), and above all Naval routine, which was based on the premise that at all times we were on board a ship at sea. The timetable therefore ran twenty four hours a day in blocks of four-hour watches. This meant that every so often one or other of us would be roused at midnight or four o'clock in the morning to go out on watch, guarding some supposedly significant installation. Non-commissioned officers, known in the Navy as petty officers, kept us up to the mark, each in his own way. 'Anyone here interested in music?' asked one of them. 'I am,' I answered brightly. 'Then move that piano over here!' Another inveigled us into a blood donation session with the promise of a 'make and mend' (i.e. afternoon off) as a reward. We never got the afternoon off, but it set me on the path of regular blood donations.

As we were nominally 'at sea' we had to keep our kit in good shape by our own efforts. We were supplied with a 'hussif' (the term is a corruption of 'housewife'), which was a cloth pouch with thick needle and coarse thread more suited to mending sails than sewing on buttons, which still serves me today. We also did all our own laundry. This was quite a task, with little equipment and fewer natural skills to pit against demanding parades and kit inspections, but we learnt a few tricks, such as running soap down the inside of the trouser crease before ironing, which effectively welded the crease into the trouser leg. We were on parade at the crack of dawn in our 'No 8s' every morning except Sunday, when we had church parade a little later in our serge suits. We had a choice of three religious affiliations: Anglican, Roman Catholic and Non-conformist. A couple of my fellow recruits were bold enough to say they were atheists. 'Non-conformist,' muttered the writer as he ticked the appropriate box, and he was right in a way. Once paraded, the command rang out: 'Roman Catholics, fall out!' A scattered group took a smart pace to the rear and doubled off behind a hut, while the rest of us stayed for a perfunctory hymn and prayer before being allowed to enjoy our Sunday leisure. Since we were 'at sea', we went 'ashore' to Portsmouth, marching out of the barracks in formations known as 'liberty boats'. We took time to get used to this curious convention, but once we did it became ingrained in us. We had absorbed some of the particular camaraderie that exists among seamen who are used to being thrown together on board real ships. In Portsmouth we would have a few drinks in a pub, uncomfortable and self-conscious in our stiff uniforms. As ratings we were not allowed ashore in civilian clothes. At another table in the pub, presenting a strange contrast, there would be an equally self-conscious group of newly-minted midshipmen in their 'issue' civilian clothes – identical blazers and flannel trousers. The midshipman is an officer cadet, so they were our age. They were officers nonetheless, and in contrast to us ratings were not allowed ashore in uniform.

In 1956, Easter Day fell on 1st April, so a mere three weeks after joining up we were given a weekend's leave. I volunteered to stay 'on board' for Easter itself, thinking it would be pleasantly quiet. It was, but I was suffering from flu, with a temperature that needed no thermometer to detect. I stuck it out as long as I could, but eventually went to the guardhouse to report sick. The duty petty officer was discouraging: the sick bay was closed for Easter so if I was ill I would be sent to Haslar hospital. According to the rules this would involve packing up my entire kit and being discharged – who knows, by the time I got out of hospital my ship might have sailed without me! He gave me some aspirin and advised me kindly but firmly to stick it out a bit longer. So it was a forlorn sentry who sat shivering on the steps of the secret installation he was supposed to be guarding that night, outsize steel helmet askew on his head and truncheon limply in his hand.

I was still Anglican enough to drag myself to Communion service on Easter Sunday, mainly for a bit of tea and sympathy. It was an odd experience. Church was the one place where public school types, both officers and National Service ratings, mixed freely, and I was both comforted by being in my element and dismayed at seeing what a narrow stratum of society was encompassed by the Church of England. I was still unwell when I took the train home the following Sunday for my compensating weekend off and gave a tetchy response to my family when, on their way to church, they serenaded me with *Rule, Britannia!* as I pulled myself wearily up the steps at St Margaret's station. I was poor company for those few days. Terrified of 'jumping ship' I was determined to do nothing except rest and ensure I was well enough to get back on time.

Our basic training continued apace and became quite relaxed. We paid a visit to Nelson's flagship HMS *Victory* and bared our heads at the spot where he was killed. I wasn't quite sure whether this was a religious or patriotic occasion, but it made me feel uncomfortable. So did the requirement to swear the oath of loyalty to the Queen. We grumbled over this, sea lawyers to a man. As conscripts, we hadn't volunteered to fight for our country, we argued, so we shouldn't be expected to swear we would die for it. Our arguments were given short shrift, and we duly took the oath. It did seem like hair splitting, even to us, but the problem returned for some National Servicemen later in 1956, when the Suez crisis broke.

By 1st May 1956 basic training was over, and we were deemed fully fledged Coders (Special). We knew we were never meant to be proper Coders, who encrypted and decrypted secret messages, and we longed to get on to the 'special' part, which meant learning Russian. The next course would only start in July, however, so the Navy had to find something to do with us over the next two months. They sent us to HMS *Mercury*, the Navy's signal school. HMS

Mercury 'sailed' over the rolling Hampshire Downs, not far from Petersfield, and would have been an idyllic place to spend the early summer, had we had something to do there. But the staff were too busy training real signallers and only gave us a few perfunctory classes. We spent most of the time on general duties. Occasionally there was absolutely nothing for us to do, so we would be handed a saw and hammer, or pot of white paint and paint brush, and told to 'look busy *and don't get caught!*' It was galling to have to creep furtively around the outskirts of the establishment following the old adage 'if it moves, salute it, if it doesn't, paint it!' while the cheerful sound of trainee signalmen beeping away at their Morse Code or clacking away to music at their typewriters rang in our ears. Happily, this routine was lifted for a time when news arrived that we were to be inspected by no less a personage than Admiral of the Fleet Lord Mountbatten, First Sea Lord and a cousin of the Queen. A frenzy of excited preparation ensued – I recall an agitated Lieutenant Commander standing over me as I desperately tried to sweep a mountain of coal into a neat pile. On the great day the Admiral strode down our ranks and stopped in front of me. I remember his face looking particularly pink, as if he had make-up on. 'Like your badge?' he barked, pointing to the Coders' symbol – a representation of an open book with a flash through it – that was stitched on to the sleeve of my jacket. 'Yes, sir!' I replied. 'Good – I designed it!' And on he strode. The job of designing badges seemed somehow inappropriate for someone of his rank, as did his childish delight in his creation. After Mountbatten's untimely death, assassinated by the

IRA in 1979, I read that he had once described himself as 'the most conceited man I know' and all was explained.

The regular ratings at HMS *Mercury* were irritated by the presence of these idle middle-class snobs among them and made fun of us. 'Hands to dinner!' boomed the Tannoy at midday, then, in mincing tones: 'Coders ... to *lunch!*' Rather more ominously, there were mutterings when yet another bespectacled Coder smugly collected his winnings at the evening's scrumpy-infused housey-housey, as bingo was then called. The Naval Police in particular, renowned for their dim wits, were convinced that the f...ing Coders had devised some way of beating the system. I was happy to take the opportunity of weekends at home, using a coach that dropped us on Friday night at the Union Jack Club by Waterloo station and picked us up on Sunday evening. I also wandered round Petersfield and sought out Broad Halfpenny Down in Hambledon, reputed to be the cradle of cricket. As often as not, however, a lovely Sunday afternoon would find us fast asleep in our mess: despite being idle during the day we still had to do various night shift guard duties and were always short of sleep.

Two months later, on 2nd July 1956, we were at last able to start serious work. We had travelled by train to the picturesque Scottish fishing village of Crail, East Fife. Our home was a sprawling complex of Nissen huts and pre-fabs that had once been a naval air station with its own runway. For the Navy's purposes it now bore the name of HMS *Cochrane*. For everyone else, however, it was the Joint Services School for Linguists (JSSL), recently relocated to Crail from Bodmin in Devon. JSSL had been established in 1951, in the coldest days of the Cold War, when the British Armed Forces found themselves chronically short of servicemen competent in Russian, the language of the potential enemy. It was a factory line for the mass production of Russian linguists, and National

Scotland's for me!
Crail Harbour, as seen in a 1960s poster, with the former JSSL a white smudge in the background

Servicemen were the ideal raw material, since they could be trained and then kept in reserve for an emergency.[1]

At last we were in our element. Our little group was joined by more naval recruits, who had been called up later but had caught up with us over the summer, as well as by contingents from the Royal Air Force and the Army. There were over five hundred students in the camp at any time, at various stages of training. As in our previous establishments, we intellectuals acted as a natural irritant to the camp's regular Service personnel. 'I think I'll have some *kapusta*,' announced one of our number, trying out his new Russian vocabulary as he eyed the cabbage waiting to be served for lunch. 'I'll give you f...ing *kapoosta*,' shot back the army cook, as he slapped an outsize dollop on the plate so that it spattered gravy all over the wretched linguist. The difference was that here we were in the majority. The camp's administration tried to maintain a semblance of military discipline among us, but it was difficult with the three Services all having different ways of drilling. We started the day by our Nissen huts at the top end of the camp parading as soldiers, sailors and airmen, then marched down the hill in increasingly fragmenting units to the pre-fabs that were our classrooms. Here, out of range of our despairing sergeants and petty

---

[1] An exhaustive history of the Services' Russian courses has been written by two former trainees: Geoffrey Elliott and Harold Shukman, *Secret Classrooms: An Untold Story of the Cold War* (London 2002). The book makes much of distinguished JSSL alumni, such as Michael Frayn and Alan Bennett. The latter wrote about his own JSSL experiences in *Untold Stories*, London 2005.

officers, we dissolved into a gaggle of students. We imbibed Russian by rote from a variety of teachers, some English, some Russian émigrés, some Poles and Balts who had washed up on our shores after the war. It was an exciting and confusing time, as we were in a new cultural environment in every sense. On a rare visit to the village in the early days I was approached by a grizzled elderly man who said something incomprehensible to me. I took him to be one of our teachers and summoned up my few words of Russian to answer him, only to discover he was a local fisherman.

Old hands said the atmosphere in Bodmin had been chummier, but that concerned me little, since within a few weeks of starting the course we were already having our ability tested. The bulk of the trainees would complete the course at Crail to become translators, but the cream would be skimmed off to do a higher level course attached to Cambridge or London Universities, eventually qualifying as interpreters. The interpreters' course had considerable attractions – a year effectively in civilian life, better pay and a commission into the officer class. It also had perils – relentless hard work and the ever-present threat of being thrown off the course if you failed two of the frequent exams. And that meant not just dropping down to the lower grade of translator, but right back to square bashing or scrubbing decks. Not everyone was prepared to take the risk, but I was, so I buckled down to my studies in preparation for the make-or-break exam. My record reads:

> 26 Sept '56. Obtained 109/125 in Major Progress Test. Selected for higher grade Russian language training at London University.

That was good, but not quite enough. We Navy people still had to be assessed as potential officer material before we started the course. We were interviewed by a panel consisting of two people we knew, the military commander of the camp and JSSL's civilian director of studies, and two we didn't, Dr George Bolsover, the lugubrious director of the School of Slavonic and East European Studies (SSEES) in London, and a Navy Captain. As we lined up for interview, those of us further down the list eagerly quizzed the first interviewees as they came out. 'The Captain gave me a hard time,' they tended to say. When my turn came I gave standard answers to Dr Bolsover and my well-rehearsed reply to the Captain's question about why I had wanted to join the Navy: grandfather a distinguished merchant seaman, sea in the blood, and so on, adding as a final flourish that I was only sorry that the long hours of study that lay ahead would prevent me from spending more time on a ship. Suddenly the Captain was incandescent. '*On* a ship?' he thundered, '*On* a ship? The ship is an officer's home and he lives *in* it! You'll be laughed out of the wardroom if you use that *disgusting* lower deck expression!' Then, witheringly: '*If* you ever get *into* a wardroom!' He subsided, but continued to fix me with a steely glare. Forewarned, I had realised that the outburst was the Captain's routine loss of temper designed to test the nerve of the interviewee, so returning his gaze I framed my reply to indicate that I felt justly admonished but in no way cowed. I could read his thinking bubble: 'Steady under fire; officer material.' I was through.

Those of us who had successfully passed through to the higher Russian courses were packing our bags again less than three months after arriving in Crail. The Navy contingent, together with an RAF group, was bound for London, some 30 strong. The Army sent their people to Cambridge. We would be not be wearing uniform in London, so we went by way of Woking, where we spent an afternoon of high merriment choosing issue civvies from a large depot. This was the mid-1950s, before open shelf department stores became common, so it was exciting enough just to walk down rows of clothing picking out what you wanted. More amazing, even to someone as unconscious to fashion as I, was the style of the clothes, which seemed to date from between the wars. The more adventurous came away dressed like Hollywood gangsters in double-breasted herring-bone suits, shirts with very long and floppy collars and trilbies set at rakish angles. As soon as possible they stowed away their issue clothes and wore their own. Thrifty as always, and mindful that clothes rationing had ended only a few years earlier, I chose a dowdy brown jacket and grey flannel trousers, which I wore throughout my time in London. I drew the line at the exceptionally prickly shirt, however, and never wore the flat cap that went with the outfit.

Our destination was Furze House, 45 Queen's Gate Terrace, a stylish frontage in Kensington. For the Navy's purposes it was called HMS *President*, although there was also a real ship of that name moored in the Thames, to which I used to report in my RNVR days.

Afloat in Kensington: Furze House, 45 Queen's Gate Terrace, from which we 'went ashore' every morning for our classes in Russell Square. Author's photograph, 2010

Furze House had been a hotel and was about as far removed as we could imagine from our barracks in Crail. It had a comfortable lounge, supplied with newspapers and magazines, and a dining room. The hotel rooms on the next three floors served as our four-to-a-room dormitories and studies. Every weekday morning, instead of the parades we had grown used to over the previous six months, we sauntered out through the revolving doors on to the streets of Kensington and took the tube from Gloucester Road to Russell Square. We struck across the Square to No 47, another elegant terrace house in the shadow of London University's Senate House.

We were welcomed on the first day by the same Dr Bolsover who had been on the interviewing panel in Crail and who, as Director of SSEES, was in charge of our course. We scarcely saw him after that. He left the actual running of the course to his deputy, Brian Toms, an austere figure with thick glasses and a Hitler moustache. Toms made it clear from the start that the course would be narrowly focused on the Russian language, written and spoken, with the emphasis on its military application. The message was repeated by our principal teacher, Mr Melechowicz, a Polish officer who had lost both hands and one eye in a grenade accident in the war, reputedly saving his comrades' lives. His scarred face, which prevented him smiling, glass eye, flat, American-accented voice and Captain Hook artificial hands all conspired to make him look like a robot. He was not – as his racy jokes in rare moments of relaxation made clear. But to begin with his very appearance reinforced the impression that our course was to be nothing but mechanical learning by rote. Happily, we discovered that most of our other teachers were women. We all lost our hearts to the petite, blonde and lively Mrs Volosevich, whose first name – Lyubov' – meant love and who could easily be made to blush prettily. The darkly enticing

Serb, Miss Gavrilović, was not such easy game. 'You English love to talk about sex,' she observed in response to some clumsy *double entendre*, then, in her most sultry voice: 'We Slavs prefer to *do* it!' That put us in our place. Our other female teachers – the cosy Mrs Chollerton, widow of a former Daily Telegraph correspondent in Moscow, the prim Miss Ivanova and the massive Mrs Alkhazova – were not of an age to attract us in the same way, but did soften the edges of the rather harsh regime we were subjected to.

Although a couple of persistent students won us the right to buy and wear the distinctive SSEES black, blue and yellow scarf, it was made abundantly clear that we were not part of the University Department. We went to none of its lectures, met none of its students and didn't even eat in the canteen, a stone's throw away in Senate House, having instead to traipse down to a Ministry of Defence establishment at the corner of Southampton Row and Theobald's Road. We were aware that in Cambridge our fellow students basked in a Chekhovian atmosphere altogether more cultured than our regime. This was largely due to the director of the Cambridge course, the formidable Professor Lisa Hill, Anglo-Russian by origin and wholly Russian by temperament.[2] Like Bolsover, she ran the University's Slavonic Department, but unlike him she involved

---

[2] 'I was a Janus, British-born with a Russian mother, thus naturally Anglo-Russian; in mind and manners British, logical and anti-worldly in heart; and by upbringing and education Russian, spontaneous, compassionate and sociable, my soul spiritual and religious but ecumenical, alert to signs and symbols, striving towards a higher plane of existence.' Jean Stafford Smith (ed), *In the Mind's Eye: the Memoirs of Dame Elizabeth Hill*, Sussex: The Book Guild Ltd, 1999, page 385.

herself closely in the Services courses as well, indeed she had been their inspiration. There was a contrast between the courses she designed, which took in swathes of Russian culture, and the more functional syllabus devised for the London courses by Toms' predecessor Ronald Hingley, with its focus on Soviet, particularly military, language and literature. There was also competition between the two. In 1952, when a mock Civil Service Interpretership Exam was set up to be taken simultaneously by the Cambridge and London courses, London had come out marginally on top. After that, an unshakeable conviction reigned in Russell Square that the London method was the better.

So it was that every day Mr Melechowicz would deal out our ration of 'BVL's and 'BNL's (Basic Verb and Noun Lists), which we would go through in class and revise at home, to be tested on the following day. In addition we would have a set book to read – four pages of complex Russian prose every evening – for which we had to make a vocabulary from our little red dictionaries. We would be tested on that too. Our first books were models of Soviet literature – Konstantin Simonov's war novel *Days and Nights*, and Yuri Trifonov's *Students*. With our third book, Turgenev's *Fathers and Sons*, one of the 19th century classics of Russian literature, I discovered the beauty of the language and never looked back.

The teaching and homework regime continued relentlessly for five days each week, but weekends were completely free, which allowed us to spread our wings. There were those who used the freedom of London to discover sex. Of an evening, while the rest of us had our noses in vocabulary lists, there was one who could often be found studying the notebook in which, like Don Juan, he listed all his conquests. He was talented enough to hold on for several months, just scraping the necessary number of marks at each exam, but eventually he departed.

I was not gregarious and never went out 'on the town' with the others, preferring to curl up in our lounge with *The Spectator*. 'The trouble with you, Martin, is that you're prematurely middle-aged!' expostulated one of the more adventurous of my fellow students. Nonetheless, accustomed as I was from my earliest school years to being one of the crowd, I rubbed along easily enough with my colleagues, one of whom, Godfrey Garrett, in the Air Force, went on to become my closest friend at university. I had my own weekend routine. I would take myself off to the cinema every Friday evening – not to see the latest releases, but to see classics: D. W. Griffiths' *Birth of a Nation* and *Intolerance*, as well as *The Cabinet of Dr Caligari*, the first modern horror film. Then on Saturday I would go home for the rest of the weekend. Sunday evenings, however, would find me and the rest of us back at our desks, mugging up for the week ahead. It was hard going, although we were not short of talent. One acerbic Oxford philosophy graduate would subject the Russian language to a logical analysis it couldn't always bear. An otherworldly academic mastered Russian so easily that he found time to study Arabic in class. And among a curiously large Welsh contingent was a future professor of Welsh.

We were of course still Service personnel and had to clock ourselves in and out, but the small administrative staff at Furze House ruled us with a light hand, wisely assuming that the fear of relegation would impose its own discipline. We wore our civilian clothes throughout, except that each day one of us had to be in uniform as 'duty cadet'. We felt self-conscious in this gear when mingling with commuters on the Tube, but more at ease sitting 'on guard' in the reception booth in Furze House for part of the evening. This duty gave us the opportunity to ogle the girls of the Women's Royal Naval Service, known as 'Wrens', as they went in and out: they occupied the other half of Furze House.

We did get the odd week's holiday. On one of them I took myself off for a painting course in Wareham, not far from my prep school in Swanage. It was a quiet and productive week, although a shade lonely – I was the only student of the artist and her disabled husband, and the only lodger at the bed and breakfast opposite their house. Every day I would go out with my easel and canvas to paint in oils on the beach or by the river Frome, my teacher coming to advise me at intervals. One day a couple of men hailed me from a rowing boat in the middle of the river:

- What are you painting on?

- Canvas!

- Have you ever tried Daler Board?

- No, what's that?

- Come and see!

This short exchange actually took the best part of ten minutes, since I found the men difficult to hear from their boat and their Dorset accent impenetrable. The upshot was that I went round to a large converted barn, where the two men, who most probably were Terry and Ken Daler, the company's founders, showed me how they were covering hardboard with cloth and coating it with a white substance to produce the effect of canvas at a fraction of the cost. I went away with a number of their boards, little realising that I was in at the birth of a cottage industry that was to grow until it took over one of the most hallowed names in artists' materials. This was George Rowney, which became Daler-Rowney and is now the leading UK company in the field. I also came away from that holiday with a sore left thumb. The sun had caught the end of the thumb that held my pallet and was therefore exposed, motionless, to its glare throughout the week.

For Easter 1957 I went to Paris for a week, inspired by one of my fellow students. I had done no preparation and with difficulty found a cheap room on the Left Bank that was only just on the right side of respectability. All the other occupants seemed to be small traders up for a motor show. I did the round of the sights, but without much joy, as I had got it into my head that Paris should only be done on a shoe string and was very mean with my eating. This was self-defeating, as I was not able to appreciate the treasures of the Louvre when my tummy told me I ought instead to be having a good meal. It was also lonely. I was usually quite happy with my own company. Being on my own was something of a luxury, living as I did most of the time in close proximity to my family or fellow students. But a week of it was a long time. Rescue came in the form of the British Embassy Chaplain in Paris, the Reverend John Morris, who had been vicar of our parish church of St Stephen's at home in Twickenham. Every Sunday he and his wife gave an informal buffet for expatriates in their flat near the Eiffel Tower, and having made my down payment by attending the evening service I repaired to it and ate my fill, enjoying chatting to the young English students, most of whom seemed to be drifting through Paris like me, which was a comfort in a way.

We were not always left to our own devices during breaks from our studies. Our respective Service authorities, worrying that our identities as sailors and airmen were melting away in the heat of the academic furnace, devised a 'back to basics' week. The Navy group pleaded to be given a week at sea, so that we would be spared the embarrassment of having to admit later in life that we had spent two years in the Navy without ever going to sea. It was administratively impossible, however, and we were sent to the Royal Naval Gunnery School at Whale Island, off Portsmouth, officially called HMS *Excellent*. The gunners at Whale Island didn't know what they were supposed to do with us, so they drilled us mercilessly every day to knock us back into shape. For me this was not a hardship – I had been drilling since the age of fifteen in my school cadet force. Our anomalous social status was harder to cope with. On arrival in London we had been promoted to Acting Petty Officers. At the time it had meant little beyond a welcome increase in pay and new uniforms – the same uncomfortable serge, but with a double breasted jacket and brass buttons. Suddenly we were among real, hardened Petty Officers. They were the backbone of the Navy, as Non-Commissioned Officers are in all the Services, and they treated us with unconcealed contempt as we huddled shyly in the corner of the Petty Officers' Mess. It was a good week to get behind us. It left one curious and slightly disturbing memory. This being a gunnery school, we were taken out one day to practise shooting with a bren-gun (a light machine-gun). I got a nasty shock from the recoil when the gun fired, but as I recovered I was rather pleased to see earth and stones flying up from the cliff face opposite, where my bullets had struck. I had a sudden urge to try again and really enjoy my feeling of destructive power. Happily, I wasn't given the chance, and the urge duly subsided.

By the summer of 1957 we had finished our course in London. Dr Toms grudgingly allowed us to sit the GCE 'A' level in Russian – this, rather than the Services' own internal exam, was the standard which meant something to us. I passed with distinction as, I think, did most of the others. It was a measure of the intensity of the course that we had arrived at this point after just a year's schooling. We were now set to return to Crail for a four or five month 'continuation and orientation course' towards our qualification as Service Interpreters.

Before we went north again we were promoted to Midshipmen. This was a major change in our Service life – we had graduated from the lower to the upper deck and needed to be able to comport ourselves as officers and gentlemen. So we were despatched to yet another training establishment, this time at Chatham dockyard. We had to learn to handle a sword on the march, which we managed with varying degrees of incompetence. The swords were big and could trip you up if not kept firmly under control. We had to take them out of their scabbards for a salute, and then put them back in the scabbards while keeping eyes straight ahead, at the risk of skewering our fingers. As 'gentlemen' we were expected to equip ourselves, and bought fine new uniforms of a soft velour material, together with an absurd little monkey-jacket, appropriately known as a 'bum-freezer', in which to dress for dinner. It was designed so that officers could be correctly dressed, but still relatively comfortable

Midshipman (Special), posing self-consciously at our family home

when dining in the confined space of a ship's wardroom. Our bow tie was designed with equal parsimony: it had just one 'butterfly' end. I could never tie it without help. I don't remember the name of the 'ship' at Chatham where we learnt these arts. It wasn't HMS *Pinafore*, like the Gilbert and Sullivan operetta, but it wasn't far off.

My second stay at Crail was thoroughly enjoyable, even though it meant braving a Scottish winter. Our living conditions were an improvement on our previous sojourn there. We were now officers and entitled to the privileges of rank. This meant a suite of public rooms ('Wardroom' for the Navy, 'Officers Mess' for the other Services) where we could socialise, with a billiard table and television. There were new faces in abundance. Our London group was joined by fellow students from Cambridge, and most evenings we would sit in a large circle around the fire alternately reading and chatting about anything that came into our heads. We were also entitled to rooms of our own. True, they could have served equally well as prison cells, but for me, who had known nothing but a shared bedroom at home and dormitories elsewhere, the privacy afforded by my own room was a luxury. Instead of queuing for our food, we were waited on by an elderly Scottish fisherman. Our palates were tickled by a choice of dishes on the menu – doubtless stipulated in the rules – although in practice there was only one item available. 'Wull ut be *fush*?' our waiter would ask, and fish it was.

The Navy still fretted over our lack of exposure to Service life, but from Crail this was easily remedied by the occasional trip to a ship berthed in Rosyth dockyard. There we would be shown the latest electronic gadgetry by technicians who assumed our 'Special' status referred to something technical and tended to punctuate their explanations with a modest: 'But you gentlemen probably know more about this than I do.' We would nod wisely, having lost the thread soon after the invariable opener: 'This is your on-off switch.' I do recall, however, being allowed to steer a mine-sweeper under the Forth Bridge, doubtless with a real sailor at my elbow.

There was nothing to do in Crail itself, and strict Sabbath observance meant that we couldn't even go to the pub on a Sunday. For that we had to go to St Andrews, sufficiently far away for us to be classed as travellers and therefore entitled to a drink under Scottish licensing laws. St Andrews was anyway our leisure destination of choice. It was just a two shillings and tuppence ('tew und tew') return bus fare away. We got to know a crowd of girls from the university. We even hit a golf ball around the famous Royal and Ancient golf course. I visited a Presbyterian church in St Andrews, out of politeness rather than conviction, as the pastor was a family friend, Charles Armour, who had been the minister of the local church when we lived in Argentina during the war, and had christened my brother Jonathan and my sister Caroline, as well as presenting me with a copy of *Pilgrim's Progress* as a prize for attendance at Sunday School. Our worlds were by now far apart, however, and we had little to talk about beyond family reminiscences.

At Crail there was none of the London tension around our studies. We had our routine Russian classes every day, but they were not onerous, and we knew that if we kept up a regular level of work we would comfortably get the qualification we were aiming for. A number of us had a more substantial incentive to keep working: we had decided to continue our Russian studies at university. I wanted to study Russian instead of French, while keeping Spanish as a second string. At some point I wrote to Dr Stanley Aston, then Director of Studies at St Catharine's College, Cambridge, to tell him of my decision. To my surprise he wrote back huffily, saying that it was not the practice of the College to allow prospective undergraduates to change the subject which had gained them admission, often in the face of considerable competition. I hadn't realised that Aston was a mediaeval French scholar and was probably upset by a prospective student escaping his grasp. All that mattered to me was that he grudgingly accepted my proposal.

The high point of our academic life at Crail, which also impinged on our social life, was the production of a Russian play. The inspiration came from a member of our Russian staff, Dmitri Makaroff. An émigré from a theatre family, he had begun producing plays (in English as well as in Russian) in the parish church at Bodmin, and the JSSL play was now something of a tradition. For us he chose *The Bedbug* (*Klop* in Russian) a satire by Vladimir Mayakovsky (1893-1930). It portrayed scientists in a future, dehumanised Soviet 'paradise' resuscitating a dissolute reveller called Prisypkin, who had frozen to death at his wedding in the 1920s, a time when private enterprise was briefly allowed to flourish. The scientists consign Prisypkin to a zoo, together with the now extinct bedbug he had had on his person, both as specimens of the insect *bourgeoisius vulgaris*. Prisypkin was played by one of our star students, Daniel Salbstein, who himself many years later resuscitated the moribund Great Britain/Russia Association after the fall of the Soviet Union. It was an excellent choice of play, allowing us all to take some part or other (I played several bit parts). We bussed in girls from St Andrews for walk-on roles to add spice to the crowd scenes, and we probably bussed in much of the audience as well – there was no local community in Crail as there had been in the historic town of Bodmin. Makaroff gave us all individual tuition in Russian pronunciation, intonation and elocution – the sort of thing we had had no time for in London and which was of lasting benefit to me. Many years later I was to bask in reflected glory when I went to Russian operas at Covent Garden and would see his name in the programme as the official Russian language coach to great singers.

It may have been to celebrate the play that we threw a party in our mess. Somebody had a recipe for a 'fruit cup' made from white wine laced with gin, and it was on this potent mixture that I first

The Bedbug

The bourgeois hedonist Prisypkin (Daniel Salbstein) is resuscitated in a sanitised Soviet paradise. The author (far left) is one of the astonished scientists.

drank myself to the point of insensibility. The following day I could vaguely recall having staggered back to my room under guidance, but I had no recollection of reappearing at the party not long after, as my friends told me I did. I simply sat in a corner 'looking like a contented frog' as a friendly colleague put it.

In February 1958 we sat the Interpretership Examination set by the Civil Service Commission. You needed eighty per cent to qualify as Interpreter First Class, and none of us made the grade. The bulk of us achieved the necessary sixty per cent to qualify as Interpreter Second Class. I came fifth in our group of twenty three Navy candidates, but we were eclipsed by the Army and RAF candidates, and my position sank to fourteenth out of the whole forty one taking the exam.

Although it was never made explicit, interrogating rather than interpreting was the job for which we were really being prepared, so to round things off we were sent on an interrogation course at the Headquarters of the Army Intelligence Corps near Maresfield, Sussex. Here we were taught that under the Geneva Conventions prisoners were obliged only to give their name, rank, date of birth and service number. The interrogator, however, without laying a hand on them, could extract a great deal more information by playing on their isolation and fear. I was temperamentally unsuited for this sort of game, and the other-worldly Arabic scholar with whom I conducted my final, 'live' interrogation at the end of the course was even more so. Our 'prisoner' was a sergeant recently returned from Cyprus, where he had been interrogating EOKA (the Greek nationalist organisation) suspects. In no time he had turned the table on his 'interrogators' and had us breaking the golden rule of never issuing direct threats or promises. 'If you tell us this or that you can have some lunch,' we pleaded, despairingly. It was our own lunch we were worrying about. When we staggered out, we found the rest of the course convulsed with laughter – as we knew, the 'interrogation' had been relayed for training purposes to loudspeakers in a neighbouring room. Our session had been a model of how not to do it, and the instructor had kept up a hilarious running commentary, correctly anticipating every mistake we were about to make. It would have been a crushing humiliation – had we felt that anything serious depended on it.

As it was, we were by that time 'demob happy', and were simply embarrassed when the imposingly named Commander David Maitland Makgill Crichton, head of the Royal Navy Section at Crail, warned us in terms verging on the hysterical about the evils of Communism. His purpose was to encourage us to join the Reserve on our demobilisation. Whatever my doubts about his assessment of the political situation – like most young people of my generation I was vaguely left wing – I was easily persuaded to join. Apart from anything else, it would mean exchanging my Midshipman's white lapel tabs for a Sub-Lieutenant's handsome gold stripe on the sleeve. I was duly commissioned into the Royal Naval Reserve (RNR). A year earlier it would have been the Royal Naval Volunteer Reserve

(RNVR) with its distinctive zigzag officer's stripes, which had given the RNVR the affectionate nickname of the 'Wavy Navy'. But the two had been merged in 1957, so I had an ordinary officer's stripe with an 'R' in the middle of the loop. Under the gold stripe I still had my thin green band, indicating 'Special'. I recall wearing this uniform for a couple of training fortnights during my university years – one back at Crail and one at RAF Tangmere in Sussex after JSSL Crail was closed. They were easy-going affairs – I needed little refreshment in Russian, which by then I was studying for my degree. I finally left the Reserve after I joined the Foreign Office. Other demands on my time had reduced the attraction of an idle fortnight's 'refresher'. More importantly, I ascertained that if it did come to war with the Soviet Union, the Foreign Office would have a prior claim on my services as a Russia specialist.

So in March 1958, exactly two years after I had joined up, my National Service came to an end. The greater part of it had been exceptionally well spent. Russian is one of those languages that starts with a steep learning curve and benefits from intensive study at an early stage – exactly what we were subjected to. I was fortunate to be able to live and work among people I would meet again and again in later years, some of whom became life-long friends. And it laid the basis for what was to prove a fascinating and worthwhile career. All this did indeed make National Service something 'special'.

Two

Spanish Interlude:
Travels with a Donkey

It was March 1958, and I still had nearly half a year in hand before starting at Cambridge. So I went to Spain to bring my Spanish up to scratch – it had been completely eclipsed by Russian. I had saved £90 during my National Service and thought that would last me a month or so while I found some work. I had an open invitation from my parents' good friends 'Hendy' Henderson, Shell's Managing Director in Madrid, and his wife Jo, with whom I had already spent a few weeks on a visit from school. But I wanted to be a bit more independent and explore Andalusia first. The cheapest method of travel at that time was by boat: for £15 I got a berth on a liner bound for Australia, which called at Gibraltar. The journey lasted only a few days, but that was quite long enough, as my cabin-mate was a chain smoker, and I woke up each morning engulfed in acrid smoke.

On the Fringes of Europe

The passengers seemed to be mainly British emigrants – this was the period when a good living could be made in Australia and Canada – but I spent most of my time with a pleasant young Pole. He was looking for any sort of work, but emphasised that by profession he was a waiter. Brought up with a fairly dismissive view of the service industry I found it hard to believe that anyone could take being a waiter that seriously.

We duly docked at Gibraltar, and I boarded a ferry going across the bay into the Spanish border town of Algeciras. It was the end of the day, and the ferry was crowded with returning Spanish day labourers, mainly female and most of them suspiciously bulky – they were loaded with contraband cigarettes. I booked into the first *pensión* (bed and breakfast) I could find, and the next day took a train to Seville. The station at Seville was bustling, noisy and awash with people hawking taxis and hotels. I walked past them, nose in the air, but once I got outside the station reality hit me: I had no idea where I was and where I was meaning to go. So I meekly returned and sought the help of a young man who offered me a cheap *pensión* and took me there in a taxi. The *Pensión Santa Cruz* turned out to be a very suitable, friendly place in the heart of Seville's historic Santa Cruz district. Round the corner was a lovely little square lined with orange trees. Seville oranges – there they were in front of me! I saw the young man a number of times after that as he brought new guests to the *pensión*. It turned out that he was a student earning a few *pesetas* to make ends meet. Thanks to him I overcame my British

Spanish Interlude

middle-class conviction that anyone hawking anything at a station was out to fleece you. This was the way services were offered in Spain at the time, and had I not learned to use them I would not have been able to go anywhere.

As it was, I travelled, mainly by train, to the main cities of Andalusia – Málaga, Córdoba, Granada, and others. Train journeys were always lively – as a rare foreigner I was an object of intense curiosity and told my story over and over again. I also ate well. Journeys were slow and long, and families on the move would bring mountains of provisions, a spinach-stuffed *tortilla* or a *paella,* bright yellow from the saffron-coated rice. Politeness demanded that if you were eating in public you should offer to share your food with strangers around you: '*¿Usted gusta?*' ('Would you like some?') was the formal question, and '*¡Buen apetito!*' the formal reply if you politely declined. But the offer was made in all sincerity, and never bringing any provisions of my own, I had no hesitation in accepting it from families I had been chatting with for several hours. The only problem was drinking: wine was passed round in a leather gourd, which you pressed to expel a thin stream of wine straight down your throat without the need for your lips to touch the spout. I found it impossible to swallow without closing my mouth (despite practice in the bath), so drinking was an embarrassment.

If I was in a provincial town on a Sunday I would go to the bullfight. This was an aspect of romantic Spain that I persuaded myself I should study and appreciate – two years earlier I had bought

On the Fringes of Europe

*At the bullfight:
the early stage, with the matador swirling his broad pink cape*

my copy of Ernest Hemingway's *Death in the Afternoon* with some school prize money. The ritual did indeed have moments of balletic beauty, especially in the early stages of a fight, when the *matador* was playing the bull with a broad pink cape that swirled away from his hips. But the part that tested the *matador's* skills, artistry and courage came at the end, when he had to play a much weakened, but somewhat wiser bull with a narrow cape in order to get right on top of the beast for the kill without himself getting lifted on its horns. His sword was supposed to pierce right to the bull's heart for a quick, clean kill, but it was my misfortune never to see this effectively done. Instead the *matador* had to finish off the bull with a dagger-like appurtenance on the end of a sword, which would cut a nerve in the neck, while the crowd would wave white handkerchiefs

Spanish Interlude

– the signal of disapproval – and hurl abuse at the luckless bullfighter. On one occasion the white handkerchiefs came out the moment the bull was released into the ring, charging and snorting impressively. What was going on, I asked my neighbour. 'Can't you see? The bull is blind in one eye!' It took me some time to get the point, as I hadn't understood the word *tuerto*, nor did the bull seem in any way unusual. But others pointed out that it was hooking only to the right. As the bull was recaptured and led out, to hoots of derision, I mused that I probably knew no more about bullfighting than a Spaniard who had watched a couple of cricket matches would know about that arcane sport, and my interest in it – unnatural anyway for someone of my temperament – began to wane.

When not travelling, I would return to my base in Seville, where my landlord kept my little attic room available. I had tried to get a job through a priest to whom I had an introduction. He advised to me put an advertisement in a local paper. I received two replies, both from young girls in Catholic seminaries hoping to find a husband. I met one of them, but it was clear from the start that my not being a Catholic ruled me out, luckily. There seemed to be no one interested in having English lessons from a native English speaker. That was hardly surprising: Spain in those days was a very poor country, and few could afford the luxury of English lessons, still less a trip to England. In truth, I didn't need a job: the exchange rate was so heavily weighted against the Spanish *peseta* that I could keep myself going in my modest style of living for many months on my savings. So I idled away my time in Seville. Jo and Hendy had given me an introduction to a young Englishman, a former Shell employee who had 'gone native': he had settled in Seville to learn the guitar, at which he was now a semi-professional. Relaxing on his flower-bedecked balcony I was captivated by his playing and determined to follow his example when the opportunity arose, which it did sooner than I expected. I should have taken more careful note of his dedication and the hours of practice he put in: the Spanish guitar is not for the faint-hearted. Otherwise I made acquaintances among the guests at the *pensión*, mainly small businessmen and technicians, who had come to the provincial capital to find the work that was unavailable in the countryside. It was a cold spring – snow had forced the cancellation of the bullfight I had planned to watch in Málaga – and we used to spend the evenings chatting cosily round a circular table in the main room, warming our feet on the brazier placed underneath it. I would have liked to hear about the Spanish Civil War, which had ended in 1939 with the victory of General Franco's nationalist forces, and about current Spanish politics. 'Fascist' Spain, at one geographical and political extreme of Europe, was the counterpart to Communist Russia at the other extreme, and these were to be my twin subjects of study at university. But conversation round the *brasero* rarely went beyond small-talk and the affairs of the day, nor should I have expected it to. These were people whose lives were taken up with hard work to earn their daily bread.

Spanish Interlude

I was waiting for Easter. I had been told I must not miss the processions during Holy Week, when the images and wooden statues of Jesus and the Virgin Mary were taken out from their churches and paraded around the city, followed by devout citizens doing various forms of public penance, some barefoot, some on their knees, some flagellating themselves. The processions would stop every so often, and the air would then be pierced by someone in the crowd, perched up a tree or lamp-post, singing a *saeta* – a fervent couplet affirming the singer's devotion. These apparently spontaneous outpourings were in fact well-rehearsed performances by well-known local artistes – I was told where to position myself to hear the best performers. Sung in a raucous voice, the music owed more to gypsy and North African Moorish traditions than to the European classical tradition. The locals knew how the *saeta* should be sung, listened out for particularly florid or difficult passages and applauded the singers who got them right. As at the bullfight, I knew that I would never penetrate the mysteries of this art form, nor did I really want to. I was more at ease in the festival week after Easter, when demonstrative penance gave way to unabashed merry-making – parades of horses and carriages carried sumptuously adorned Spanish beauties around the city, while ordinary mortals caroused for night after night. I joined them, along with my friends from the *pensión*.

On the Fringes of Europe

Seville, Easter 1958: carousing

One of my acquaintances, an electrician whose name I have long since forgotten, invited me out of the blue to join him on a visit to his family in the countryside. It was a day's journey. We went by train to some remote railway station and waited for hours at a fly-blown café for a passing car to take us to an even more remote village clinging to a mountainside. I had no idea where it was and will never find out. As the car wound up the narrow roads I saw the reality behind the clichéd phrase 'scratching a living from the soil' – peasants bent over their hoes working the terraces they had cut out of the mountainside. I was probably the first foreigner to set foot in the village and was an object of unconcealed curiosity as I was paraded at the local café. Where was England? I tried to explain that it was across the Channel, but that didn't help, as the Spanish *La Mancha* also refers to the area south of Madrid that was the home of

Spanish Interlude

Don Quixote. 'So England is as far away as Madrid', mused my interlocutors

The electrician's family were nothing if not hospitable, and I had to decline nervously his wife's offer to wash my clothes as she cheerfully pummelled the life out of his at the stream that rushed past their house. They were not in fact local people and had lived until quite recently in one of Spain's North African enclaves – Ceuta or Melilla. Listening to radio broadcasts from their former home was their evening entertainment. They could only do this when there was electricity in the village, which came on for an hour or so every evening. They would unscrew the light bulb from the single source of electric power and screw in the radio lead instead. With my arrival they found a new entertainment. I had brought my electric shaver, which could also be run off a light socket, and the evenings

Clinging to the mountainside:
The unknown village in Andalusia

would be spent with the shaver doing duty on one grizzled beard after another while I looked on apprehensively, wondering whether Remington's technology would cope with this sort of punishment. The technology of the mud-floored house clearly didn't run to an inside toilet, but I also searched its surroundings unavailingly for an outside earth closet. Eventually I had to ask the grandfather, who reassuringly took me by the arm and led me out to the wide open spaces of the mountainside. 'The whole mountain is your toilet,' he said, with a lordly sweep of the arm, and proceeded to explain to me the varying properties of the greenery available to wipe your backside with. The young brother-in-law of my electrician friend was also hospitable and took me out for a brandy at the local bar, where I made an unpardonable mistake. Aware of the family's extreme poverty, I sneakily paid for the brandies he had ordered, the cost to me being almost too small to calculate. He was understandably upset – I was his guest and he would pay, never mind the cost. But he didn't bear a grudge and told me a lot about life in this poverty-stricken part of Spain. I was fascinated, but frustrated, as my Spanish wasn't really up to his local dialect.

One day we paid a visit to relations in a neighbouring village. We set out on foot, a party of half a dozen or so with a donkey. Everyone took turns to ride the donkey except for my friend's wife, heavily pregnant, who as far as I could see neither requested, nor was offered a ride. I held back out of a mixture of politeness and fear, but was eventually persuaded to mount the donkey for the last stretch of the journey. The donkey trotted briskly along the ancient path, so deeply worn into the side of the mountain that its edges were at waist height for the walker and grazed my knees as I squeezed them into the bulging flanks of the donkey. I was terrified that the path would narrow to the point where we got stuck, but after a while we emerged on to a broad plain, and I saw farm buildings ahead. The donkey knew that was our destination and speeded up. We were by now far ahead of the rest of the party, so the farmer and his family were confronted by the puzzling sight of a familiar donkey with an unknown, pale-skinned, bespectacled youth on its back. With true Spanish hospitality, however, they took us in and gave us refreshments, while I did my best to explain who I was and where I had come from. There was much laughter and re-telling of the story when the rest of the party arrived, and we had a glorious picnic on the sunny hillside.

Towards the end of April it was getting stickily hot in Seville, and I abandoned the city to take up my open invitation from Jo and Hendy Henderson in Madrid. A Cambridge lecturer, Dr Aguirre, who happened to live in the same set of rooms as my brother Robin, had given me an introduction to an academic friend of his in Madrid. The purpose was to see if he had any ideas for a job for me. Again there was nothing doing on that front, but he kindly gathered a few friends and invited me to tea. Courteous but reserved, this group listened politely as I babbled away about my adventures in Seville and its surroundings. They winced at my fake Andalusian accent, with which I thought they would be impressed. They then told me rather sternly that what I had experienced was not the real Spain at all, but the hybrid that had developed from centuries of Moorish occupation before the Moors had been expelled in the 15th century, with a strong gypsy admixture, the whole romanticised by French writers and composers, typically Bizet in his opera *Carmen*. The real Spain, austere and high-minded, was to be found in Old Castille, across the mountain range north of Madrid, in such cities as Salamanca, León and Burgos. This is what I should be exploring. Chastened, I retired to unlearn my atrocious accent, but the home comforts offered by Jo and Hendy in Madrid easily won out over my cultural appetite, and beyond a couple of day trips to the historic cities of Segovia and Ávila I never took up the recommendation of the academics. Indeed, the longest trip I did with Jo and Hendy, together with the British Vice-Consul Stanley Croft and his wife and an American couple, was a drive through old haunts down to Gibraltar, but taking in the desolate area around Murcia on the Mediterranean coast, officially classified as desert.

Jo and Hendy had an airy and spacious house at the top of a hill on what was then the outskirts of Madrid. Trams would labour up the hill and turn right with a deafening screech just before they reached the house. Opposite the house across a sandy expanse stood a bar called *El Ruedo* (The Wheel), which I photographed and painted, but never patronised: in Madrid I became a gentleman, and

Spanish Interlude

it wouldn't have done for me to frequent the sort of bars that had been my normal habitat in Seville.

Jo and Hendy were a delightful blend of opposites. She was Irish, diminutive, a bundle of energy, a dedicated doer of good deeds and active in her local Catholic church. She constantly searched for enlightening things for me to do. She would arrange Saturday excursions, using the office car and chauffeur. Poor Hendy felt obliged to come too, although he liked nothing better than to potter around at home doing some carpentry or sitting under a tree sipping *maté*, a staple tea-like drink from Argentina. A large man, slow of movement, from a Protestant family and with a flat northern accent, he could look a shade morose until his moon face dissolved in an enormous smile, which it did when he was involved in his favourite occupation of mixing cocktails behind the bar that he had constructed himself for their home. Jo and Hendy had always got on well with my parents, whom they resembled in many ways, but my father, an avid devotee of the classical music repertoire, could never understand how alongside Verdi's *Otello* they could also enjoy *Annie Get Your Gun!*

I was fascinated by their lunchtime routine. Hendy would be driven back from the office for the long lunch break, and during the meal they would do *The Times* crossword at breakneck speed, one reading out the clue and the other providing the solution instantaneously. Hendy would then sit placidly at a table and play a

The Shell manager's residence:
Jo and Hendy's house in Madrid

A guitar concert in the garden given by Jo's teacher and his wife:
Hendy in the centre, Jo far right

Spanish Interlude

couple of hands of patience before subsiding on to a nearby couch, from where his gentle snoring would be heard within seconds, no matter what else was going on in the room. Then up and back to the office.

Among her many activities Jo had taken up the classical guitar, which was enjoying a revival in Spain and elsewhere under the influence of the great guitarist Andrés Segovia. I had been enthused by my visit to the young English guitarist in Seville and took lessons with Jo's teacher. I was soon thinking of taking a Spanish guitar back to England with me. Ample as my funds were, they didn't stretch to buying a guitar, and I begged a loan from my father, which of course he generously agreed to. In due course my teacher, a craftsman as well as a musician, made me a guitar of my own. I spent every spare moment on the guitar, and for a decade my flute went into a bottom drawer.

On my visit to Madrid from school in 1955 Jo had organised a medical student, Manolo, as a Spanish-speaking companion for me. Manolo and I may have met once or twice during this second visit, but we were going our separate ways, and in any case there was a powerful counter-attraction in the person of Carmen Galante. Carmen taught the Hendersons' younger son Andrew at the Anglo-American school in Madrid (their older son John being at boarding school). She had become a close friend of Jo and Hendy and spent much of her free time with them. Ten years older than me, so about thirty when I met her, she was a stunningly attractive Spanish beauty, with fiery temper and winning charm in equal measure. Although her English was almost faultless (she had been educated partly in England) she was kind enough always to speak Spanish to me. I was of course completely in thrall to her and happy enough to be seen around in the company of someone who turned all heads. Carmen's family history had been tragic. Her father, an army general, had been assassinated in the mid-1930s during the turmoil that led up to the Spanish civil war of 1936-1939. The family (Carmen had a brother and at least one sister) fled to North Africa, where her mother died – of grief, Carmen asserted. It must have been at this point that Carmen, orphaned in her early teens, was sent to school in England. In Jo and Hendy she found a surrogate family to give her the warmth and security she had been robbed of in her own.

Carmen was formidably clever. Although she taught languages, her strong subjects at school had been physics and chemistry. Socially she was highly conservative, but in spirit fiercely independent, a combination that stood her in bad stead in the Spain of those days. She had been planning to marry a Spaniard in the conventional way. This meant a long engagement, during which she and her fiancé would see little of each other. Shortly before the wedding Carmen learnt to her horror that her fiancé already had a family. When she confronted him, he made no attempt to deny it, but airily said that he had planned to give them up on marriage,

Spanish Interlude

Sailing to England:
Carmen, cigarette in hand, as always

assuming that this would be enough for Carmen. It wasn't, and Carmen instantly dismissed her fiancé and with him her prospects of a normal married life in Spain. She liked to be admired by men, however, and had a string of young, mainly English, devotees (as I was to learn to my disappointment), who could be kept at a safe distance.

When the summer heat reached Madrid it was time for me to go back home. I had been recommended a pleasant route by boat from Vigo, the capital of the province of Galicia, in the North West corner of Spain. I was flattered when Carmen, who had separately decided to give up her job and spend some time in England, elected to join me for the journey and use my parents' house as a base for a while. I was peeved when we found ourselves on the train and boat with two young men, Argentine and Spanish, to whom Carmen devoted as much attention as she did to me, but relieved that they were on hand

On the Fringes of Europe

to absorb some of her fury at the accommodation she had been given on board. I had booked our passages and without thinking had chosen the cheapest option, as I always did. Carmen was not rich, but she had an acute sense of her class – and it was not steerage. She managed to upgrade herself, but worse was to follow when on our arrival in England the Customs officer at Southampton gleefully and maliciously went through every item in her suitcase. At Waterloo Carmen was met with a large bouquet by another young man – a forlorn English admirer. To give him due attention and allow Carmen to calm down before meeting my parents we repaired to the Surrey Tea Rooms, a genteel establishment that adorned the Waterloo station of those days. I was apprehensive, as Carmen was still in a foul mood when, together with the Argentine, who had nowhere to go, we took the train home. I needn't have worried. As the taxi from Richmond drew up outside my parents' house Carmen switched on her irresistible charm, handed her bouquet to my mother as if she had bought it specially for that purpose and won my father's heart with a glance. Nor did Carmen's incessant smoking diminish her appeal.

Carmen stayed with us for a while, and to a certain extent my parents took over the role in her life that Jo and Hendy had played in Madrid. She made no secret of the fact that she wanted to marry and settle down, but it had to be with the right person. She found him in the end, an American lawyer, with whom she settled happily in Houston, Texas.

Spanish Interlude

I still had plenty of time left in that long summer of 1958 between National Service and Cambridge, so I took a job as a messenger at Shell's head office, at that time in the City. This was where my father worked, and he must have been the one who told me that Shell took on students in the summer months to cover for holidays. On my first day I was surprised to find that I was driving a lift – there was an urgent need to fill a week's gap. I say 'driving' advisedly, as in those days it involved more than pressing buttons. The lift did stop automatically at the right spot on each floor if it was going slowly enough, but you had to ensure that the speed was right by operating a large wheel with a handle on it: turn the wheel to the right to send the lift upwards – the further to the right the faster it went – and to the left to send it downwards. So if you hadn't gauged the right speed for the lift as you approached each floor it would either shoot past or stop short, requiring it to be inched up or down till it reached the point where the doors would open. The weight of the passengers in the lift was a crucial factor in the calculation, and in my first few days I was all at sea with it, earning a black mark for shooting straight past a Shell director because I had just deposited a large load in the basement canteen and had forgotten how light the empty lift would be for the return journey. To make matters worse I was suffering from sleeplessness: at night I would feel my legs being alternately compressed and elongated as my body reproduced the motion of the lift. By the end of the week I was beginning to get the hang of it and even to enjoy joking with my customers about my uncertain skills as a lift operator. But by the beginning of the next week I was assigned to more conventional messenger duties, as had originally been intended. This meant collecting, sorting and delivering papers to the appropriate offices, where I emptied the occupants' out-trays and redistributed their papers. I had never seen work in an office before and was baffled by what these serious men, with piles of paper to the left and right of them as they sat, were actually doing. I plucked up the courage to ask one of them, who sat behind a door labelled 'Co-ordination Department'. 'I ... er ... co-ordinate,' he replied. I even penetrated as far as my father's office once, although he was well off my beat. There he was, equally serious behind his piles of paper and quite unlike the man I knew at home. I remained baffled, little imagining that I would spend the bulk of my career doing the same thing.

I found my fellow messengers rather craven towards authority. One of them was scandalised when I casually asked someone coming along the corridor to open a door for me as my hands were full with a large tray of coffee and crockery for a meeting. 'Didn't you realise that was Mr Watson, a Department Head?' he whispered. But he added to comfort me: 'He's a real gentleman, he won't have minded.' I should have realised that as a 'college boy' I could afford my lackadaisical approach. My colleagues, mostly ex-servicemen and policemen in their early fifties, would not easily have found another job had they irritated their bosses at Shell.

Spanish Interlude

My 21st birthday on 12th August 1958 passed quietly. I hadn't wanted to plan anything in case I was still in Spain at the time. In any case, a major family event was coming up, my older brother Robin's wedding on 23rd August. His bride Mary was the daughter of Sydney Caffyn, of Caffyns Ltd, the prominent car dealers in the south of England, and a former mayor of Eastbourne. So the wedding was a big event, reported in the local press. After years of post-war penny-pinching, it was also the first occasion when our family splashed out: morning suits for the men, hired from Moss Bros, and seats in a Pullman Carriage – the stylish, art-deco luxury carriages with their brown livery that were attached to the service down to genteel Eastbourne. I went back home on Sunday, a day earlier than the rest of my family, as I had to start work at Shell at the usual time on Monday morning. One of Mary's younger brothers, Robert, tried in vain to persuade me to stay on and join him on his commuter train early on the Monday morning: it would take us straight up to the City in good time. Lackadaisical as I was about my work, I was ultra-conscientious about starting on time and didn't want to take the risk of being late. My caution may have saved my life: Robert's commuter train was ploughed into as it stood at Eastbourne Station, a few minutes late, by a steam train carrying cars and passengers from Scotland, running a few minutes early. Four people were killed, and Robert suffered serious injuries, from which it took him years to recover. The accident cast a shadow over a model family occasion.

On the Fringes of Europe

Nearly half a year had passed since I had finished my National Service, and I was more than ready to start at Cambridge. I had put Spain back on my map, though I never really got under its skin, as I did later with Russia. But there was a strange affinity between these two countries at opposite ends of the geographical and political divide in Europe. Russia and Spain both encompassed extremes of climate and regional variation, and both had extreme political systems. And the inflexible, absolutist governments of each were in the end unable to maintain control over their volatile populations.

All dressed up: the Nicholson men at Robin's wedding.
From the left: Dad, Robin, Martin and Jonathan

Three

Cambridge 1958-1961:
Following in the Family's Footsteps

I went up to St Catharine's College, Cambridge, in October 1958. My father had graduated from Cath's in 1930 and Robin in the summer of 1956. I was next in line. So it was with a sense of routine rather than achievement or expectation that I set foot in one of England's two most prestigious institutions of higher education.

Robin, in the middle of his Cambridge PhD, had smoothed the way for me in practical matters. He had bought me a second-hand bicycle and a suitably tattered undergraduate gown – you didn't want to look like the 'freshman' you were – and fixed me up with lodgings. As important, he and his wife Mary provided me with many a good meal at their appropriately named Far Cottage up the Girton Road.

On the Fringes of Europe

The collegiate system, which separated social from academic life, looked to me just like the house system at my boarding school. But I never felt the same sense of family at Cath's as I had at Bramston House, Oundle. Sport was again supposed to embody the spirit of the College – doing something sporting was all but mandatory. I had finally reconciled myself to the fact that I was no good at ball games and restricted my activities to athletics. Having failed to make my mark in middle-distance running I joined the College cross country team, a small group of not very inspiring individuals who, like me, didn't shine at the more prestigious sports. One or two of them ran prodigious distances in training, and I was proud to complete the 23-mile Cambridge Boundary Run, for which I was rewarded with a 'Bounders' tie, but I was not prepared to run that sort of distance regularly and developed a self-serving theory that it took a being of lesser intelligence to pound mindlessly along mile upon mile of road.

St Catharine's could only accommodate a few of its undergraduates: rooms in College were a privilege reserved for your second or third year. Nor did the College in those days have additional halls of residence. Freshmen had to find lodgings. Robin fixed me up with his former landlady, Mrs Johnson, whose husband, universally known as 'Johnnie', was one of the College servants. This was something I was not well prepared for. It meant that after the formal evening meal in the College Hall – the one mandatory event of the day and known simply as 'Hall' – I had to leave the

Cambridge

company of people I was just getting to know, get on my bike and cycle off to Harvey Goodwin Avenue, a mile and a half away, for a solitary evening of 'study'. The inverted commas are appropriate: despite having kept my mind hard at work during my National Service I was still accustomed to following a well-defined programme with frequent tests. I came from an educated but not scholarly family and had little idea of how to set about any sort of intellectual enquiry of my own that involved 'reading widely', as we were encouraged to do. I had acquired a coffee making machine and imagined myself in my little sitting room in front of the fire, deep in books. The truth is that I soon dozed off. I didn't have a radio and would have been fearful of disturbing Mr and Mrs Johnson with it if I had. They, meanwhile, would sit in the back room of their 'two up, two down' terrace house with their radio turned low, fearful of disturbing me.

I was, in fact, wasting a precious opportunity. I should have been going to some of the many evening lectures on offer, or to the cinema or theatre, or even deliberately 'wasting' my time in the pub. But I was still, in my school slang, a 'swot', feeling the need to spend every available moment mugging up on my core subjects. These were Russian and Spanish, shared in equal measure in Part I of the Modern and Mediaeval Languages Tripos.[3] Each had its

---

[3] The term Tripos is said to have originated with the three-legged stool on which a Cambridge Bachelor of Arts would sit to conduct a humorous debate with candidates for degrees. Now it simply refers to the Cambridge degree system.

separate faculty, so the overall direction of my studies, such as it was, lay with the appropriate Fellows of St Catharine's College. My first port of call was my Tutor, the genial geographer Augustus Caesar, imaginatively so named by his father Julius, but known to all as Gus. 'I am in charge of your moral welfare,' he said with a twinkle in his eye, having quickly assessed that I was not likely to cause him much trouble on that front. He handed me over to the Director of Studies, Dr Stanley Aston, the man who had reacted badly to my request a year earlier to change from French to Russian. A soldier-scholar, his brusque manner seemed to owe more to his war service in the Intelligence Corps and his involvement with the Territorial Army than to his study of mediaeval troubadours. He summoned our group of freshmen linguists, told us to map out a programme of lectures we thought we should attend and then ruthlessly cut it by a half. Lectures, he explained, were just a relic of the days before books could be mass produced. We could advance our learning much more quickly by reading. There was logic in his advice, but for me it was misguided, since I needed the breadth provided by a lecture more than the depth of a book. True, some lecturers were perfunctory in their task – I and my fellow students were incensed once when a lecturer, having searched his briefcase, confessed that he had forgotten his notes and promptly walked out with a mumbled apology. Had he nothing to say to us beyond what was written on the paper in front of him? But I also remember an absorbing series of extra-curricular lectures on the history of philosophy.

Cambridge

At the Slavonic Faculty, tucked away somewhere near the station, I found myself surrounded by so many familiar faces from my National Service days that I felt I had just returned to JSSL Crail from a week's leave. The impression was strengthened by the unexpected presence among us of a Major Collins from the JSSL military administration. Had he been sent to Cambridge to keep us in order? No: he had been 'bowler hatted' – made redundant – as the Armed Forces were being drastically reduced in size. National Service was to end in 1960 and JSSL Crail was to be closed down at the same time. Although at Crail Major Collins had had nothing to do with the Russian language, he had become intrigued by it and was funding himself for a university degree from his redundancy payment. I admired his humility: a married man with two children, he quietly took his place among us youngsters who just a few months previously had been expected to salute him and call him 'sir', but now strutted around, arrogantly displaying our superior knowledge of Russian. He buckled down regardless and came out three years later with a First and a teaching job at a worthy school.

I was the only undergraduate in Cath's reading Russian, so I teamed up for supervisions with Godfrey Garrett, in Sidney Sussex College, with whom I had been through the London and Crail Russian courses. Godfrey and I became firm friends. He had a wild and adventurous streak, which led him into girls' bedrooms at the dead of night and up mountains, from which he would fall off spectacularly. He was a first class all-round sportsman, and it was after one of his mountaineering accidents, with one leg encased in plaster, that he beat me soundly on the squash court. I never asked myself at the time why we two opposites should be drawn together, but I suppose I got a vicarious thrill out of his adventures, while providing him with an emotional sheet-anchor. It was Godfrey who persuaded me to join a skiing party to Sauze d'Oulx in Northern Italy run by the travel agency Inghams. It was led by Andrew Bache, who later became my flatmate and played a crucial role in getting me a job in the Foreign Office. Skiing holidays were primitive affairs by today's standards. For most of us the attraction lay in meeting the opposite sex at the mysterious ritual called *après-ski*. I was apprehensive and kept pestering Godfrey in vain for information, particularly about the dress code. 'When I go skiing, I go to ski,' he replied sternly. In the event, he wasn't able to: another broken leg (or perhaps the same one) put him out of action.

The head of the Slavonic Faculty was Professor Elizabeth Hill, whom I knew by repute from my National Service days. I brought with me all the prejudices against her with which I had been imbued when I was on the rival course to hers in London. Her first lecture confirmed them. 'Russia in the Nineteenth Century was like a giant Christmas cake,' she intoned. 'There was a thin layer of icing on top – the nobility; a huge mass of suet underneath – the peasantry; and in between – the *marzipan* layer of the *intelligentsia*.' Lisa Hill's

Cambridge

Gently does it:
skiing at Sauze d'Oulx, 1959

unctuous tone put me off, and for some reason the 'marzipan layer' stuck in my gullet. Emboldened by Aston's robust attitude to lectures, I struck her off my list. I was probably the loser, as I needed a general framework, however fatuously presented. My only memory of her after that was at a Faculty production of a Russian play, throughout which she chatted to her neighbour – a Russian characteristic with which I was to become familiar. Lisa had reached the height of her career and no longer seemed to care much about ordinary undergraduates.

I should have been more tolerant of Lisa's unctuous tones. I discovered that this way of speaking was a rather Russian characteristic when the Faculty entertained the Russian/American author Vladimir Nabokov as a visiting lecturer. In those days

On the Fringes of Europe

Nabokov's very name set off a frisson, as *Lolita*, his shocking novel about a middle-aged man's sexual involvement with a twelve-year old girl, had been published only a few years previously. But Nabokov talked to us in his plummy voice about Nineteenth Century Russian literature, making the case that the censorship of the Tsarist era was relatively benign – if you didn't like it you could keep quiet. The Soviet State, by contrast, demanded output, of whatever quality. He illustrated his point with an apocryphal story of a local writer/bureaucrat who reported smugly to the Soviet Writers' Union: 'In the pre-revolutionary era there was only one member of the Tula Section of the Writers' Union – Lev Tolstoy – but now in Soviet times we have twenty five members!' Our next visiting lecturer was just such a writer/bureaucrat, Aleksei Surkov, who as Secretary of the Writers' Union in the late Fifties had tried to stop publication of Boris Pasternak's Nobel Prize-winning novel, *Doctor Zhivago*. Surkov's lecture was a collection of platitudes that made me wonder why we in the West felt it necessary to entertain these Soviet time-servers at all. It was a question that came up many times in my later experience of cultural exchanges with the Soviet Union, and the answer was always the same: better to keep some sort of dialogue going than none at all. It was unsatisfactory, since part of the bargain in our own minds was that we would use the occasion to challenge these Soviet officials and their ideology, but we were always far too polite to make an impression on Surkov and others whom I met in later years; they were masters of evasive tactics.

Cambridge

Cambridge had not adjusted to the higher standard of undergraduates reading Russian in the late Fifties, most of whom were fresh from the Services course: the Russian papers for Part I of the Tripos were pitched quite low. Many of us came away with a First at the end of our first year. I was among them and was rewarded with a College Exhibition and a small bursary that reduced the fees my father had to pay for me. I was pleased on his account, as educating his children was a burden, and also on my own. I was always conscious of the element of family connection in my entry to St Catharine's: the First and the Exhibition rid me of the nagging feeling that I wouldn't have qualified on my own merits alone.

Spanish was more troublesome than Russian: it's an easy language for beginners, but a difficult one to master. But whereas with Russian I was on my own in the College, with Spanish I had the support of two others, Tony Murrell and Dick Long, with whom I was later to share rooms. The three of us would toil up the long road towards Girton College on our bicycles, gowns billowing in the wind, to our supervisions with Florence Street, wife of Dr John Street, who was later to supervise me in Latin American Studies. I got an Upper Second in my Spanish Part I. With the first part of the Tripos behind me after one year, I had two years for the more serious business of Part II, which would result in a final BA degree.

The question that really interested us was what we would do on our first Long Vacation. I decided to join a few of my fellow students as a courier, taking tourist groups to Spain. Mass tourism outside the UK was just getting under way in the late 1950s. The Costa Brava, running north of Barcelona to the French border, was the first stretch of Spain's Mediterranean coast to be developed for this new market, and Swan's Tours (before they went up-market and became Swan Hellenic) were among the first British companies to exploit it with package holidays. Swan's recruited language students for the summer season, both as representatives stationed at their resorts and as couriers to escort the tourists there and back. By nature a settler rather than a traveller, I was inclined to apply for a post as representative, but vacancies were limited. I was anyway persuaded that this was the tougher option – you could never get away from your charges. So, having again irritated Stanley Aston by announcing rather too airily that I was planning to go down a few days before the official end of term to start work, I found myself with Tony Murrell at Victoria Station one Sunday afternoon under the tutelage of an experienced medical student mustering a group of some two or three hundred tourists bound for Spain. Swan's offered the cheapest route – a gruelling thirty-six hour journey by train and ferry, to which many tourists added an overnight journey from Scotland or the north of England: this was before the age of budget or charter flights.

I did the round trip nearly once a week over two months, and the worst part was always greeting the arriving tourists at Victoria. 'Mr Swan!' they would call, recognising our distinctive blue blazer with its swan badge on the pocket: 'Where's our seat?' In the sticky summer heat we longed to get our heavy blazers off our backs, but didn't dare, as at any moment the real Mr Swan, who owned the business, might turn up to check how things were going, and he was particular about the blazer.

Our train from Victoria took us to Newhaven, where we boarded an overnight ferry to Dieppe. From there we went by train to the north side of Paris (Gare du Nord), by coach to the south side (Gare St Lazare) and by overnight train down to the French border with Spain. This was the most demanding, but also the most satisfying section of the journey. Our tourists had vouchers for an evening meal, but the Wagons-Lit restaurant car couldn't possibly have coped without us couriers marshalling our charges into two or three sittings, helping to clear tables and sometimes even lending a hand as waiters. Our reward was a delicious meal in the calm of the evening provided by the grateful Wagons-Lit staff. Experienced couriers would then regale us new-comers with disaster stories of entire carriage loads of Swan's tourists being uncoupled by mistake and shunted off to a siding in the middle of nowhere. This sort of thing made me anxious, but an experience during my very first trip gave me an unshakeable and justified confidence in the French railway system and its staff. One of our party wandered off at Gare St Lazare and was missing when our train drew smoothly out of the station at the appointed time, punctual to the second, without any of the whistle blowing and agitated 'Hurry along there!' that we were accustomed to in the UK. There was nothing we could do beyond informing the guard. I was astonished when in the dead of night the missing traveller stumbled into the very couchette compartment where I was snatching a couple of hours' sleep. He had boarded the wrong train and found himself hurtling off to destinations unknown. The railway staff had identified a station along the route through which his train would pass before ours, took him off the first train and pitched him into ours. He spoke not a word of French, like almost all our tourists, for many of whom this was also a first experience abroad. 'Mr Swan, they won't take English money!' was a regular cry when our train made its first morning stop at a station in the south of France. 'What would you say if someone in Paisley tried to pay you in French money?' was my stock reply, which usually found its target.

At Cerbère, the end of the line for the French train, as Spanish railways ran on a broader gauge, we would pile out of the train, walk across the border to Portbou and get on a rickety Spanish train that would trundle slowly down to Barcelona. Once arrived, we couriers would hand our charges to the resident representatives, who would take them on to the various coastal resorts, while we made our way wearily to a little flat rented by Swan's to accommodate couriers between trips.

During our few rest days I made little effort to get to know Barcelona. Apart from catching up on sleep, my main aim was to eat well at no cost. For this I would travel out to the resorts where

Swan's put their clients – Blanes, Tossa de Mar and Lloret de Mar. The hotels there would willingly offer Swan's personnel free meals as a reward for the good business they did. I would then log the real cost of the meal on my expense claim form – the first and last time in my life I have fiddled expenses. This was an accepted practice to boost our ludicrously small basic wage. In my embarrassment at this piece of deceit, I made a feeble joke about it the first time I presented my claim form, and was met by a very cold stare from my superior – I should have realised that the practice could only continue so long as nobody so much as hinted at its existence. In Barcelona I spent my time at the Café De Brasil on the city's famous Ramblas, sipping sherry and chatting up the attractive barmaid. She tried to teach me some Catalán. The language struck me as a hybrid of Spanish, French and Italian, but I was told firmly that it was in fact older than all three. I bought myself a text book, but never made much headway with it. There was little practical advantage in those days in learning Catalán – we were still in Franco's Spain, 'One, Great and Free' (*Una, Grande y Libre*) where regional aspirations and languages were suppressed. After these few idle days we would pick up a party of returning tourists and do the journey in reverse.

I was heartily sick of the courier job by the time the season ended and looked forward to getting back to academic life. For Part II of the Modern and Mediaeval Languages Tripos we had to choose five papers out of a long list. I chose three Russian papers: Russian

On the Fringes of Europe

History since 1800; Russian Literature and Thought since 1800; and a paper on the novelist Ivan Turgenev (1818-1883). I was crafty in choosing three papers focusing on the Nineteenth Century, arguing speciously that they were mutually reinforcing. My real reason was that the material overlapped and therefore saved me work. It would have been wiser to delve more deeply into Russia's Eighteenth Century or mediaeval past, or even study the origins of the literary language through Church Slavonic, the Russian used in church, as Oxford undergraduates were obliged to do. But like many others I assumed that Soviet Communism was there to stay, that it represented Russia's 'end of history' and that the key to understanding it lay in the turbulent Nineteenth Century when revolutionary ideas developed. My lack of depth told many years later, when Communism collapsed and Russia itself tried to find a new identity based on its own history rather than the alien ideology of Marxism.

My supervisor for the literature papers was a lugubrious don from Emmanuel College, E. R. Sands. He had served in the Navy during the war, where he learnt Russian. He interpreted on the Arctic convoys that ran between Britain and the Soviet Union and had been spell-bound by his Soviet fellow interpreter, who whiled away the hours on watch by reciting Pushkin's *Eugene Onegin* by heart from beginning to end. After the war Sands had been recruited straight from the Navy by Lisa Hill to teach on the Services Russian course she was setting up in Cambridge, and from there he got a lectureship in Lisa's department. Meticulous to a fault (we once spent an entire supervision hour trying to define 'poetry') he had little time for his mentor's broad brush approach and considered her to be a dilettante. She had published a 'stressed text' (i.e. a text with the correct stress marked on each Russian word) of a book we were reading, and I once asked in all innocence why the stress marks came to an end after the second page. Sands responded with malicious glee: 'Lisa's enthusiasm ran out after the first couple of pages – making a stressed edition isn't that easy, you know!' He had reason to say so, as he himself was frequently mocked for having produced no scholarly work beyond a stressed text of Turgenev's most famous novel, *Fathers and Sons*, a copy of which I saw a decade later proudly displayed at the Turgenev country house and museum outside Orel in Russia. However, the ponderous Sands suited me better than the effusive Lisa, as did the rather dry Ian Young, who supervised Godfrey Garrett and me for the history paper. I was taken aback when he announced he was giving up his lectureship to take a translating job with the United Nations in Geneva. It was such a mundane sequel to a Cambridge lectureship! But, he explained, he had a family to support, and the money in Geneva was so much better.

I chose two Spanish papers: Spanish Discovery, Conquest and Settlement in Mexico from 1490 to 1580; and a paper on Cervantes, author of *Don Quixote*. This was a good choice. The history paper, for which I was supervised by Dr John Street, gave me an insight not only into Spanish imperial attitudes but also the Aztec civilisation that they clashed with. Reading *Don Quixote* in full and in the original was more fun than I had ever expected it to be. Once I had got the hang of it, the archaic language of chivalry, the Don's pastiche of it and Sancho Panza's pastiche of his pastiche had me laughing out loud. But I struggled through Cervantes' final work, *The Labours of Persiles and Sigismunda*, of which he said: 'It is either my best work or my worst ...' It was his worst, but like the Russian writer Gogol, whom I was studying at the same time, Cervantes was concerned not to leave a satirical work as his legacy: he wanted to be remembered for a more uplifting story. Gogol had the sense to destroy his sequel to *Dead Souls*, but Cervantes left a rather tedious romance, which demonstrated what can happen to a great writer when he tries too hard.

I had little contact with my supervisor for Spanish, Dr John Boorman, Fellow of King's, one of those bachelor Cambridge dons who inhabited an intellectual world of his own. He once asked me, oblivious to my limited intellectual horizons, if Cervantes' short stories reminded me of the early Japanese novel. I didn't know the Japanese wrote novels, let alone early or late. He was often to be seen striding through the colleges lost in thought, an unkempt figure accompanied by, or accompanying, an equally unkempt dog. I once heard Boorman hammering away at a piano composition of his own at the Music Society's monthly concert – it baffled even serious musicians.

Cambridge

I had upset my landlady Mrs Johnson by leaving her lodgings in search of rooms, whether in College or not, where I would have a little more contact with my fellow students. Together with Dick Long I was fortunate enough to be allocated a suite for the two of us in the Woodlark Building in College. These were not the prestigious rooms overlooking the quadrangle, but were more modern and convenient: we had a joint sitting room and facilities and our own rooms at either end of the suite, so we could be as sociable as we liked. Dick was the person I spent most time with in the College, but we were no longer studying Spanish together. For Part II Dick took up Arabic, in which he became deeply absorbed. His later career as an Arabist to some extent paralleled mine as a Sovietologist: he served as Embassy Information Officer in various Middle East posts and then joined the British Council, where he also found the time to write several books on Middle Eastern history.

By this time I had formed a circle of friends, without belonging to any of the established groups who sat together in Hall. I recall the geographers, the theology students and above all the actors, who were quite adept self publicists. The least conspicuous of them was Ian McKellen, now the renowned Sir Ian, perhaps most widely known as Gandalf, from *The Lord of the Rings*, who seemed a shy and rather grey figure. But someone told me I should go and see him in Harold Pinter's *The Birthday Party* at the Cambridge Arts Theatre. His performance simply overwhelmed me with its power and poignancy.

On the Fringes of Europe

*Among future stars: from the St Catharine's 1958 Freshmen photograph.
I am one row down from the back, second from the right. Next but one on my right is Ian McKellen, and one from the left in the back row is Tim Waterstone, founder of the bookshop.*

For my second long vacation, the summer of 1960, I was more inclined to follow Stanley Aston's advice and do some serious reading. I knew that I lacked the self-discipline to do this at home, so I came back to college for the Long Vac Term. This extra term was more or less compulsory for scientists, who couldn't take their laboratories home with them, but less common for arts undergraduates. Having decided to avoid anything that dealt directly with my subjects, I studied among other things Karl Marx's *Das Kapital* (without actually reading it, but reading Isaiah Berlin's rewarding critique of Marx). Still further removed from my degree subjects was James Joyce's *Ulysses*: I made sense of it because at the same time I was attending a series of extra-curricular lectures by the eminent Joyce scholar David Daiches. I managed a game of tennis every afternoon with three fellow undergraduates of equally low standard. And I passed my driving test. I had booked myself eight lessons and a test, to the annoyance of my instructor, who reckoned it was his prerogative to decide when I was ready for the test. But I had a domestic imperative. After much agonising, my parents had finally bought a Morris Minor Estate with its classic wooden coachwork from Caffyns, the family firm of their daughter-in-law. (Its Brighton registration was UUF, so it and my parents' subsequent cars all became 'Goofy'.) My father had a driving licence, preserved from the time when they could be obtained on application, but he couldn't drive because of his history of epileptic seizures. So my mother, in her 50s, had decided she would learn and was busy taking lessons. In the mean time the car was in Cambridge, in the care of Robin. The idea was that I should drive it home at the end of the Long Vac Term, becoming the family chauffeur until my mother had passed her test. I had some extra coaching from Robin in Goofy, a scary experience, as this car's clutch was a lot livelier than the driving school's, and we did alarming kangaroo hops in Cambridge's narrow streets while I was getting used to it. But my greatest good fortune was that on the afternoon of the test those same streets were deserted: the shops were shut for Wednesday afternoon's 'early closing' and a downpour had driven the cyclists off the road. 'If you don't pass today you never will,' said my instructor, half encouragingly, half ominously. I did, and a few days later I was driving myself back to Twickenham. Passing the test did not mean I had mastered the art of driving, however, so it was a tense three hours or so I spent on the road. So tense that it temporarily suppressed the hay fever from which I had been suffering – my arrival home was marked by a prolonged fit of sneezing as the tension relaxed.

Before the start of my final year I decided I had time for a cycling expedition to France. I had conceived the romantic idea of cycling to Rheims in late September, staying in youth hostels and earning a little pocket money by harvesting grapes for champagne. My brother Jonathan generously lent me his racing bicycle in place of the staid 'sit up and beg' model on which I had toured in France a few years earlier and which I considered too juvenile. I was wrong: the thin tyres of the racing bike made cycling over the cobbled streets of French towns agony. A more serious mistake was to plan the French aspect of the trip meticulously while ignoring the fact that I had many miles to cycle in England before reaching Lydd airport in Kent, from where I was to make the short hop by a shuttle air service to Le Bourget. Having set off at the crack of dawn on a Sunday morning without a map I completely lost my way going out of London towards Kent and didn't arrive at Le Bourget before the afternoon. It was evening by the time I had found my Youth Hostel and a *Les Routiers* café, where I was served a meal so generous that I had far too much to eat and drink and passed a very uncomfortable night. I had set myself a target of more than 100 kilometres per day, and by the time I reached Rheims I was too ill with stomach pains to do more than buy myself a train ticket and come straight home. The first person I met on the train was a Swan's courier. His immediate comment – 'You shouldn't have bought a ticket, you should have spoken to me first!' – only added to my humiliation.

So in October 1960 I went up for my final year in a somewhat depressed mood, with the beginnings of a peptic ulcer and on a diet. It was all forgotten after a few weeks, and I had an enjoyable year, now in a room of my own on the other side of the quadrangle, working steadily towards my final exams. In the 'Prelims', I had again got a First, which was all the more valuable as it included Spanish, my weaker subject. Cambridge didn't work on a modular system, however, and the results of one's preliminary exams were not 'banked' in any way. So everything depended on the few days in May 1961 when I tackled in quick succession the five papers I had prepared for Part II. I was at home when the results came through, but Dick Long read them on the notice board outside the Senate House and phoned them through to me: he had got a First; I an Upper Second. For a moment I was envious of him and disappointed with myself, but it soon passed. I didn't feel like a first class scholar and knew that I hadn't used my time at Cambridge to best advantage. Besides, I was in good company: most of the fellow undergraduates whom I knew, including Godfrey Garrett and Tony Bishop (with whom I was to be associated throughout my Foreign Office career) got an Upper Second like me. So did Roger Bartlett and Tony Briggs, both of whom went on to become professors.

Nonetheless, I felt, and still feel, that my years at Cambridge were not spent as productively as they might have been. This is a common enough experience – how many graduates regret spending so many of their university days carousing and so few working? For me it was the reverse. I knew that I had to work hard and get a good degree to justify the sacrifice my father was making to send me to university, but in doing so I missed out on many of the intellectual and social opportunities that Cambridge offered. In some ways I felt I hadn't really earned the prestigious degree I had been awarded, and I didn't want to pay the princely sum of £8 to upgrade my BA to an MA. Then as now the MA was conferred by right to holders of a BA after a lapse of two years. I knew several graduates (some of them respected lecturers) who had nobly stuck with their BA, rather than increasing their qualification without doing any more work. But I succumbed to pressure (and a bit of blackmail) from my father – he insisted he would pay the £8 if I didn't. Ever the dutiful son, I couldn't bear to see him disappointed in me over such a small affair.

It was only in the next stage of my student life that I broke free. I had an exciting year in Moscow in prospect. Under an Agreement on Cultural Exchanges, negotiated in 1958 between the British and Soviet Governments, each country was to send to the other a group of graduates for an academic year. The British Council, which organised the exchange on our side, selected me as one of the group for the third year of the agreement's operation, 1961-62.

Cambridge

Master of Arts:
this degree day photograph was taken on 20th March 1965, following my travels abroad

I remember little of the selection process, except that the interviewing panel once again included the ever present George Bolsover, who had stared at me gloomily in Crail in 1956. His presence was reassuring, and I had little difficulty in presenting and defending the subject I had chosen for my studies in Moscow: *Soviet Criticism of Cervantes*. It combined my Russian and Spanish disciplines, and I knew that Russians had always been interested in Cervantes' immortal creation, Don Quixote: 'quixotic' ideas were very much part of their intellectual heritage. Ivan Turgenev, the subject of one of the papers for my Part II, had examined the contrast between thinkers and doers in his essay *Hamlet and Don*

Quixote; Anatoly Lunacharsky, the first Soviet Commissar of Education, had illustrated the role of the individual in history in his play *The Liberated Don Quixote*; and Soviet critics struggled tirelessly to portray Cervantes as a revolutionary ahead of his time. It didn't matter that I had no intention of pursuing the subject beyond my year in Moscow. The point was to make a reasonable case for getting to Russia and putting my five years of academic study into context.

Four

Moscow University 1961: Enjoying the Thaw

One of the luxuries of my student days was the pause for relaxation between one event and the next. In the summer of 1961, before doing my post-graduate year at Moscow University, I had time for a five-week Italian language course organised by the British Institute of Florence. I had long wanted to get beyond *Che gelida manina!* ('Your tiny hand is frozen!') and other gems from Italian opera, and this was my chance. We had our classes in the relative cool of the morning under an energetic teacher who surprised me – in the heart of historic Florence – by singing the praises of my home suburb of Twickenham, where she had once done a course. 'Ah! Strawberry Hill!' she would sigh. True, Florence was by comparison impossibly hot and noisy, and I was glad to escape it at weekends perched on the pillion of the Vespa

On the Fringes of Europe

scooter that a fellow student had enterprisingly ridden all the way from England. *Andate piano, eh!* ('Drive slowly, won't you!') said my worried landlady as we set off for San Gimignano with its fourteen mediaeval towers, Siena with its huge central square, big enough for the annual horse race, Pisa with its leaning tower, or another of the jewels of Tuscany. Despite these distractions, Moscow was beckoning all the while: I picked up a copy of Boris Pasternak's banned novel *Doctor Zhivago*, which had been smuggled out to Italy and published in the original Russian. Truth to tell, it was far too difficult for me to take in while lounging by a public swimming pool in Florence.

Back home in late summer, I immersed myself in mundane but important preparations for Moscow. My mother made me an ingenious winter coat out of my father's old overcoat lined with an equally old coat of hers made of squirrel fur, turned inside out so that the fur formed the lining. It caused some amusement in Russia (and problems in cloakrooms, of which more later) but was extremely warm. It did however lack the broad, fur-lined collar that looks so impressive on Russian great-coats, especially military ones. I had always thought the collar was there for show, but experience taught me otherwise: a few months later my unprotected face would freeze in the bitter cold.

I also had some affairs to settle on the other side of the Atlantic with the Brazilian authorities. My parents were British, but I had been born in Brazil. In Brazilian eyes this made me a Brazilian citizen and thus due for National Service in my 'home country'. The British and Brazilian governments had, however, reached an agreement in 1955 that British citizens who had done their National Service in the UK could go straight into the reserve in Brazil. It took me endless visits to the Brazilian consulate in London to get the process sorted out. The official concerned, a Mrs Braune, affected not to understand why neither I nor my parents had an address in Brazil (we had left more than a decade ago, in 1946), why I had allowed my Brazilian passport to lapse and why I didn't have Brazilian *cruzeiros* to hand to pay some administrative fee. Eventually the process was finished, I swore an oath (in Portuguese) to 'defend my country with my life' and was rewarded with an impressive certificate assigning me to the Brazilian Navy as a 'First Category Reserve'. When I complained about the bureaucracy to a Cambridge acquaintance who had been through the same process, he was surprised. 'But you did give Mrs Braune chocolates, didn't you? She loves chocolates!' That was a lesson I learnt too late. I was also too punctilious in informing the consulate that I wouldn't be able to turn up in person in December 1961 for my annual report, as stipulated in my certificate, since I would be studying in Moscow. Some months later the consulate phoned my parents: 'How can he be in Moscow, when Brazil has no diplomatic relations with the Soviet Union? When he comes back he will have to pay a fine!' I never did pay that fine, or show my face in the Brazilian consulate again, which means, I suppose, that somewhere in their archives I am shown as a deserter.

The British authorities, for their part, were preoccupied with the Cold War. As a British student going to Moscow I came into their field of vision. One morning I was jerked out of my preparations by a letter from an official addressed to me in my naval rank and summoning me to what was still the War Office for an interview. Was this some sort of call-up notice? The official quickly disabused me by blandly announcing that the War Office venue was just cover and that he was an Intelligence Officer. His service was interested in impressions gathered by British exchange students during their time in Moscow. They would not be asking me to do anything illegal or dangerous, just keep my eyes and ears open while in Moscow and have a chat with them on return. My natural instinct was always to respond positively to requests for co-operation from people in authority, so I was surprised to hear myself saying 'No', without hesitation. I didn't want to be encumbered with this sort of task, however simple it might appear.

We set off for the Soviet Union on Monday, 11th September 1961. Tension between East and West was running even higher than usual, and not for the first time the touchstone was Berlin. Although deep inside Communist East Germany, the city was still nominally controlled by the four allies who had been victorious in the Second World War: the Soviet Union, the United States of America, Britain

Moscow University: Enjoying the Thaw

and France. Berlin's 'four-power' status was jealously guarded by the three Western Allies, which guaranteed a certain freedom of movement between the eastern and western zones within the city. In 1961 East Berliners were fleeing in ever greater numbers through this gap in the 'Iron Curtain' behind which the Soviet Union had otherwise successfully imprisoned Eastern Europe. On 13th August the East German regime stemmed the tide by building a wall between East and West Berlin. This was the notorious Berlin Wall, whose collapse twenty eight years later signalled the end of the Communist regime behind it and the whole East/West division of Europe. The building of the wall was a challenge to the West on the scale of the blockade of West Berlin imposed by Stalin in 1948. Then, the Western Allies had rescued the West Berliners by mounting a massive air lift of vital supplies. On this occasion there was nothing in practice the West could do to help the East Berliners. The wall had been built in the Soviet Zone, so any attempt to interfere with it would have carried the risk of war with the Soviet Union. I knew nothing of what counter-measures were contemplated, but our student exchange scheme seems to have been put in question. At all events, our Soviet visas only came through during our final briefing on the eve of our departure, and I well recall the relief on the faces of the British Council officials in charge of us when they did. Nor, of course, did I know at the time that ten years later I would play a small role as interpreter in the East/West negotiations that led to a temporary halt in these perennial Berlin crises.

Under the circumstances it was not surprising, as my siblings told me many years later, that my mother was depressed by my departure – she feared she would never see me again. But my family were buoyed by seeing a photo of four of our group of students in *The Times* on the following day: going to Russia for a year still made news. And very soon my weekly letters started rolling in, which reassured them that I was living in a civilised, if rather different, country. It was relatively easy for my parents to picture me in Moscow, as we had a common point of reference: a beautifully written, sensitive book, *My Russian Journey*, by Santha Rama Rau, an Indian author who had paid an extended visit to the Soviet Union with her American husband in 1957. My letters are peppered with allusions to the book.

It took us the best part of a week to get to Moscow. We took a Soviet steamship for the five-day trip to Leningrad. The *Baltika* had been built in 1940 in the Netherlands for the Germans, seized by the Soviet Union as war reparations, named the *Vyacheslav Molotov*, and in 1957 given a politically neutral name following the former Soviet Foreign Minister's political demise. Just a year before we set off, in September 1960, it had been taken off its humdrum duties to convey the Soviet leader Nikita Khrushchev to the United Nations General Assembly in New York, and the first thing we noticed on boarding was a large blue plaque commemorating Khrushchev's 'Voyage of Peace'. His visit was remembered in the West less for

Moscow University: Enjoying the Thaw

From The Times of 12th September 1961

Mary Harris became Professor Mary McAuley, a noted expert on the Soviet Union, and I was later to live alongside Bob Evans when he was Reuters correspondent in Moscow.

the onset of peace than for Khrushchev's banging his shoe on his desk at the UN, a piece of bad manners that was concealed from the Soviet public for decades.

The atmosphere on the ship was convivial. Yevgenii, the Entertainment Officer, tirelessly organised us into various group activities. I didn't realise at the time that Yevgenii was using these activities to get to know us. A year later I was on board the same vessel on my way to Finland and again met Yevgenii, who questioned me closely on what I and my fellow students had been doing meanwhile. By that time I could recognise that he was a KGB (secret police) officer and his job was to provide an early report to his authorities on these young and impressionable people who were about to spend the best part of a year under their gaze.

We students got to know each other as well. I shared a cabin with Brian Murphy, a straight-talking Ulsterman who was to become one of my longest standing friends. He was some fifteen years older than the rest of us and was already established as a lecturer in Russian at Sandhurst. We were mostly straight from University – Cambridge, Oxford and London. The only one I already knew was George Walden from Cambridge. I had looked down on him as someone who had come straight from school and therefore had difficulty knowing which syllable to stress in Russian words, not having undergone the rigours of the National Service course. But I learnt to respect his intellect when he effortlessly demolished an essay I had written on Dostoevsky's *Idiot* in a literary criticism class and then came away with a First. He was to be a close colleague in my early career at the Foreign Office before he climbed to greater heights and went into politics, becoming an MP and junior minister. The other Cambridge graduate was Roger Bartlett, who was also to become a firm friend and my window on the academic world.

Our first port of call was Rostock in East Germany. It was also my first view of life behind the Iron Curtain and on brief acquaintance a good advertisement. But our guide on the coach taking us to the town centre was utterly cynical, telling us of the shortage of potatoes and how ridiculous it was to have an election campaign (which was in full swing) when there was only one party

Moscow University: Enjoying the Thaw

to vote for. It turned out he was originally from Hamburg and had moved to East Germany because that was where his wife came from. Now he was stuck there and sickened by it. He was quite happy for us to throw him English papers over the side of the ship in full view of the People's Police, claiming that they dared not put people like him in prison because it wouldn't leave enough to carry on working. This was the first intimation of many I was to have over the years that so-called 'totalitarian' states are seldom as rigidly controlled as outsiders imagine, or indeed as their own rulers would like to think.

Our second, and rather more attractive, port was Helsinki, but I was even more impressed by Leningrad (which has now reverted to its original name of St Petersburg), where we docked in the evening and found the wide streets and classical facades all floodlit. We were met by Marcus Wheeler, a young member of staff from the British Embassy in Moscow, whom we were to get to know better during our stay, and I better still when we worked together in the Foreign Office Research Department a couple of years later. We left four of our number in Leningrad, while the remaining fourteen went on to Moscow by train, travelling in a luxurious 'soft' carriage. The Soviet Union was officially a 'classless' society and so could not admit to dividing passengers into First and Second Class, but the authorities were not prepared to give up their own privileges on that account, so they simply re-categorised railway carriages as 'soft' and 'hard'.

On Lenin Hills: the imposing skyscraper that served as home for a year

In Moscow we were taken to the ornate tower block that was to be our home for the next nine months. It was one of seven similar blocks built towards the end of Stalin's life with the express intent of putting Moscow on a par with the major cities of the capitalist world. Set on the Lenin Hills (which have now reverted to their original name of the Sparrow Hills) at the south-west extremity of the city, high above a bend in the Moscow River, it was an imposing sight – the tallest building in Europe at the time. I was less in awe of its architectural peculiarities than of the challenge it presented to someone trying to find his way around: it was an anthill, where all the other ants seemed to have their predetermined routes. In time I was to develop my own, but initially I frequently found myself in the

Moscow University: Enjoying the Thaw

wrong sector of a building whose four 'Zones' exactly matched each other. My Zone was 'G', my room 819, which meant it was on the eighth floor. More precisely – 819 *left*, as the door of 'block' 819 led on to two small bed-sitters with a shared toilet, wash basin and shower. It was well designed and would have done justice to many a university campus in Britain. Only gradually did I come to realise that accommodation of this standard was a rarity even in favoured Moscow, still less in the USSR as a whole, and that our colleagues in Leningrad (and later in provincial Voronezh) had a much rougher deal.

A further challenge was that Moscow was huge and slow-moving. In my early letters home I constantly complained of the amount of time it took to get anything done. While our home was on the Lenin Hills, not all the university faculties had moved up to join it; the Philological Faculty, to which most of us were attached, was still in the centre of town. It was good to be able to enjoy the elegant old University building on the historic Moss Street (*Mokhovaya Ulitsa*) – that being the street where people used to buy moss to stuff in the cracks in their wooden houses. But *Mokhovaya* was a good hour away by bus or Metro. It could take a further ten to fifteen minutes simply to get across some of the six-lane streets, including a long walk to find the nearest pedestrian crossing. Moscow was always jam-packed during the day, which made moving around a slow business. It was not the lively bustle of city life, rather a dense stream of sullen individuals. Public transport was always crowded, and a polite request to move further down the bus might easily end in a furious argument or even a fight among the tired and overwrought passengers. I was told that a good half of central Moscow's day-time population would have come in for the day from the nearby countryside to shop for essential goods not available locally (including foodstuffs that they may have produced themselves, but which had been commandeered for the pampered capital). And we had to get used to the notorious 'three queue' shopping system, under which you first queued to ascertain the availability and price of the item you wanted, then at the cash desk to pay for it, and then again at the first counter, receipt in hand, to collect your purchase.

We made things worse for ourselves during our first few days by going around in a gaggle. To an extent this was necessary. We had to present ourselves *en masse* at the Foreign Department of the University to get vital documents: a pass to the hostel – for this is what the great 'Stalin wedding cake' was still called, since that was the only purpose it served – and foreigner's residence permit, the only document Soviet authorities would recognise. We went as a group to the British Embassy for a briefing by the Cultural Attaché and a reception given by the Ambassador, Sir Frank Roberts. But a crowd of fourteen trying to locate a Moscow restaurant for a quick meal led only to frustration. We soon found our own eating routines. Most of us abandoned our British habit of eating two meals during the day in addition to breakfast, and moved closer to the Russian practice of eating just twice a day – *zavtrak*, which dictionaries translate as breakfast, but can be eaten at any time in the morning, and *obed*, dinner, which can be eaten at any time in the afternoon or early evening. I developed a taste for the processed milk products that loom large in the Russian diet: buttermilk, sour cream and cottage cheese. A mixture of these with some bread, taken first thing in one of the hostel's canteens, often together with Brian Murphy, another early riser, would set me up for most of the day.

A number of us who worked at the Lenin Library in the centre of town used our privileged entry to the House of Friendship (*Dom Druzhby*, of which more later) to have a good lunch at its canteen. It was relatively expensive and frequented more by the 'gilded youth' – children of the Party elite, conspicuous by their Western clothes and cigarettes – than by ordinary Soviet citizens. But we British students were well off by Soviet standards. The Soviet Ministry of Higher Education paid us the normal rouble stipend for graduates, but this would have been scarcely enough to live on. We also drew from the British Embassy a generous top-up in roubles provided by the British Council, which ensured that we could live comfortably. The British authorities were clearly anxious that we should not run short of money and be tempted down the dangerous road of selling our valuable Western possessions illegally on the black market.

Otherwise I learnt to snack when the occasion presented itself – an open sandwich in the interval at the theatre, a doughnut or an excellent ice cream (on sale year-round) from a street kiosk, or that emergency roll and cheese stored in the 'larder' between the inner and outer window panes of my double-glazed room, ready for when I came home late with an empty tummy. We all found ourselves on occasion knocking hungrily on each other's doors late at night in the hope of something that would keep us going till the morning.

We also had to discover our own laundry solutions. There was a laundry service, but every article delivered to it had to be securely labelled. I was sure I could cope with the gargantuan wash room deep in the basement, where hundreds of students, enveloped in steam, toiled over primitive washing machines. Had I not done all my own laundry in the Navy? The machines weren't quite as primitive as I thought, and I earned a severe ticking off from the woman in charge when I up-ended mine in an attempt to empty it. I gave up and sought the services of one of the many elderly ladies who haunted the corridors. Some were cleaners; others were mothers or grandmothers of students, living in the complex illegally, having sneaked in without a pass. Eventually I found one who did all my laundry for a few roubles. I didn't ask where she did it. We learnt of one American student whose shirts were laundered regularly, but returned only after two days. He eventually discovered that his enterprising laundress was washing and ironing his shirts on the first day for her son to wear, then washing and ironing them again to give back to the American.

We were responsible for cleaning our own rooms, which were inspected every so often by a Sanitary Commission. With my naval

Moscow University: Enjoying the Thaw

experience behind me I was well versed in the art of keeping clean those parts that inspectors check to catch out the unwary – tops of doors, cross-struts under beds – but I was not familiar with the cockroaches and bedbugs that were endemic in all Soviet buildings. In the event I was troubled by neither, but was once rudely awakened from a nap by a posse of three burly women in white coats armed with spray guns who shouted *'Klopy yest!?'* ('You've got bedbugs!?') before spraying the entire room. It may have kept the beasts at bay; it certainly forced me to evacuate my room for the rest of the day.

I had been studying Russian intensively for five years, but I had never seen a Russian of my own generation in the flesh and was surprised when I did. I wasn't prepared for the number of students at the university who suffered from physical defects. Like me, they would have been children during the Second World War, but unlike me, most would have been under-nourished and many would have been at starving point. Their war-time suffering was under-played in the propaganda about the brave new world they were creating, but they were quick to cite it if ever we were to draw attention to their low standard of living.

The first young Russian I met formally was Volodya Dushkin, living in the other half of my 'block' G819. A stocky country lad, he was in the final year of his German course. When we first met we did some ritualistic ideological sparring, which Volodya decently brought to a halt after a suitable period by concluding that we had simply been brought up to think differently. Like so many Russians I was to meet, he envied my extensive travels and thought I must enjoy special privileges to be able to do so. Again, like so many Russians, he was keen to get my opinion on his English pronunciation. I handed him my copy of James Joyce's *Dubliners*, from which he read surprisingly well, so I gave it to him. At that point we rather solemnly agreed to call each other by the 'familiar' rather than 'polite' form of address. Despite that, we didn't see much of each other, although we lived cheek by jowl, and it was only at the end of the academic year that we had another heart-to-heart talk. I overheard Volodya sighing and groaning rather theatrically in his room (the walls were paper thin) so I asked him what the problem was. 'Happy is the man who marries a girl from Moscow!' he intoned solemnly and explained that final year students were desperately hunting down Muscovites of the opposite sex to marry so that they could get a coveted Moscow registration and continue to live in the capital when they had finished their compulsory four or five year assignment elsewhere. Volodya had been unlucky and saw himself condemned to a life of teaching in the provinces, which were as boring for Soviet Russians as they had been for Chekhov's *Three Sisters*. He had been fortunate in getting his education in the capital, perhaps on some rural quota system, but he hadn't been able to maintain his toe-hold.

Moscow University: Enjoying the Thaw

The foreigners in the hostel were scattered among Russian students, which meant that casual contact was easy. A student of English might approach us for instant language tuition or to seek our opinion on his or her essay. 'Is it *correct*?' they would ask insistently, while we tried in vain to convince them that our liberal education didn't divide literary criticism into correct and incorrect. Other students simply engaged us in conversation on the landing, where the lifts disgorged their passengers and where we all did spells of duty manning the telephone at the reception desk. We knew that they had to report our conversations to their authorities, but it didn't cramp our style.

I was sought out by a student of Spanish, Valentin, who had learnt that there was a Spanish element in my subject of study. He was somewhat tedious company, insisting that we always spoke Spanish together, but he kindly invited me to his aunt's house in the picturesquely named village of Elk (*Los'*) on the outskirts of Moscow. This area near Moscow did indeed contain some of these large animals. There I met and took a fancy to his cousin Rita, who was studying Swedish and lived in the girls' dormitory in the central tower part of the hostel. I remember her now less for a romance that never blossomed than as an example of the moral maze in which Russians of her generation had to find their way. She berated me for enjoying a film that was all the rage, *And What if it's Love?* The film showed the tender emotions of teenage lovers winning out over the strict canons of their teachers. This was not what the Soviet Union was about, she maintained, and as an antidote took me to see *Chapaev*, an iconic mid-Thirties film about a heroic Red Army commander from the civil war that followed the Russian revolution. Rita was an activist in the Komsomol, the Young Communist League, and would in due course join the Communist Party. But it turned out that her family's history had been far from the ideal. Her father, a factory manager and senior Party official, had been incarcerated in Stalin's labour camps for ten years on false charges. 'Why after all this are you thinking of joining the Party?' I asked, bemused. 'It's in the blood,' she replied simply. Her personal sense of right and wrong left me uneasy as well. I once admired a handsome Swedish/Russian dictionary on her shelf and noted that it was long overdue from the library. 'Oh, I told them I'd lost it,' she said, making clear that she now considered it hers. 'But that's a lie!' I exclaimed. 'All Russians lie, Dostoyevsky said so,' she replied, as if that clinched the argument. As time went on I found more and more of my acquaintances had no hesitation about lying shamelessly and convincingly. Whether or not this is deep inside the Russian psyche (I never found the Dostoyevsky reference, the existence of which other Russians have hotly denied) I came to realise that Russians of my generation were the children of people for whom lying was often the only way to survive in the Soviet Union. Why admit to your bourgeois or aristocratic origins if this was going to deny you an education, or worse? And of course their leaders were engaged in the biggest lie of all, that they were building a uniquely prosperous society.

Moscow University: Enjoying the Thaw

There were other groups of students from the West and the Third World whom we got to know: a small group of serious Americans on a similar exchange to ours; some less serious Scandinavians; and a noisy group of Italians. The last were all Communists, but would complain louder than any of us 'capitalists' about the awfulness of the Soviet system. We teased them about this, but they had an answer: 'If the Russians can make the system work at all, just think what we Italians could do with it!' There was a lone Indian, also a Communist and virulently anti-British, but scrupulously polite towards us individually. He made his name among us through an unforgettable incident when he came back from the shop in the basement of the hostel in a furious temper. He had once bought two bottles of milk. There was a small refund on each bottle, so he took them both back, but only bought one new bottle. The shop refused him a refund on the second empty bottle unless he bought a second full bottle. Unwilling to do so, he realised that he was burdened for ever with an empty milk bottle on which he would never get his refund. 'Believe me,' he thundered, to the delight of us British students, 'when we have Communism in India, we will not lose our English tradition of liberalism!'

There was another group of British students in Moscow at the time. They were members of the Communist Party of Great Britain, and the Soviet authorities kept us well apart. They were studying at the Soviet Communist Party's clandestine Higher Party School to improve their theoretical grounding. The scheme was not a success.

Soviet officials criticised the British comrades' lack of interest in the theory of Communism, while the British Communist Party leaders were not interested in the production of Party workers who spoke Moscow jargon. All this is revealingly described in the memoirs of one of them, Jim Riordan, who went on to make a successful academic career in the UK as an expert on sport in Soviet society.[4] Riordan's memoirs also throw light on the privileges enjoyed by the elite, with their special shops and sanatoria, in this allegedly equal society. Our own insight into the world of privilege came when one of our group was unlucky enough to lose a prominent false tooth and his handsome features with it. The university polyclinic duly put him in the long queue for a replacement, but seeing that he was a Westerner and therefore had money, surreptitiously slipped him the details of a private dentist, who turned out to have a fully equipped surgery behind the modest door of her flat. The polyclinic doubtless got their cut of the proceeds.

Before arriving in Moscow I hadn't been very interested in Soviet politics, which seemed a world apart from the philosophical arguments of the nineteenth century history and literature I had studied at Cambridge. I knew only that there had been an easing of the political atmosphere since Stalin's death in 1953. But the events of 1961 lit a spark. On 12th April, Yurii Gagarin had made the first

---

[4] James Riordan, *Comrade Jim: the Spy who Played for Spartak*, London 2008

manned flight in space. His picture was all over the place, and shortly after our arrival it was joined by hundreds of red flags, acres of red bunting and slogans hung across the streets in honour of the impending 22nd Congress of the Soviet Communist Party. To the horror of conservationists, a glass and concrete 'Palace of Congresses' was built within the Kremlin walls to host the delegates, with all the fittings imported from the West to ensure its quality (gents' toilets by 'Standard' from the UK, I proudly noted when it later opened as a public concert hall). Despite the cracks in the system that were already showing in Eastern Europe, Soviet self confidence was at its height, and Khrushchev used the Congress to push through a Party Programme promising Soviet citizens that in twenty years' time they would be living under Communism. To Western ears, 'Communism' was a spine-chilling word, but to the Russians it spelt utopia. According to the Party Programme, the Soviet economy would overtake the American economy in ten years, while in twenty there would be an abundance – fairly distributed – of everything that was currently in short supply, principally food and housing. Some Russians took the whole thing at face value. One balmy evening as I was walking back to the hostel I overheard a young couple behind me earnestly discussing the Programme: 'No, Sasha, the free distribution of food only comes in the *final* stage of the building of Communism ...' But for most people the gap between the Programme and their daily life was just too obvious for the Programme to be taken seriously. Their reaction was indifference and scepticism, which found expression in the political jokes that circulated round Moscow. The vehicle of these jokes was often the mythical 'Armenian Radio', to which questions were addressed, such as:

Q: What is the name of Khrushchev's hairstyle?

A: *Harvest 1961* (Khrushchev was completely bald, and the poor 1961 harvest matched it).

As the year drew to a close, food shortages even hit Moscow. 'As well as running out of eggs, Moscow ran out of milk and butter for a few days last week,' I wrote to my parents on 3rd December. In the following year, on 1st June 1962, the price of meat and butter was suddenly raised by 30%. My normal lunch now came to one and a half times its usual price. It didn't mean all that much to me, but for Russians, who had been led to believe that food prices would go down, not up, it was a cruel blow. There were some spontaneous demonstrations in the provinces, and in the southern Russian town of Novocherkassk the armed forces were called in. They shot into the crowd, killing 23 people. Initially, none of this was reported in the papers, but word was passed round. 'Where did you hear about it?' I asked the Russian student who gave me the news. 'Radio Station OBS,' he replied with a straight face. 'What station is that?' '*Odna Baba Skazala* (An Old Woman Said …).'

Moscow University: Enjoying the Thaw

It was not, however, the widening gap between ideals and reality – a slow-burning fuse – but the final dethronement of Stalin that brought the Party Congress to its dramatic end. After a series of impassioned speeches against the former leader and his colleagues (apart from Khrushchev himself, of course, who choreographed the performance) a motion was carried to remove Stalin's mummified body from its place beside that of the undisputed leader of the revolution, Lenin, in the Mausoleum on Red Square. Quite by chance I found myself there with a Russian friend on 2nd November 1961; a large crowd had gathered to see the last boards of a temporary hoarding being hammered into place around the mausoleum to shield the undertakers and engravers from prying eyes. A week or so later the mausoleum reopened with just the name LENIN engraved on the marble and with Stalin re-interred under the Kremlin wall alongside other revolutionary leaders. Similar temporary hoardings started going up all over Moscow in places where there were statues or portraits of Stalin. I had only just started taking an interest in them as works of art and wrote to my parents on 26th November:

A sad thing I noticed yesterday – my favourite mosaic of poor old Joe in one of the Metro stations – he is dressed in his postman's uniform holding a sheaf of letters (or is it corn?) and wearing a comic smile – has been boarded up and presumably will soon be there no longer. It is quite fun making little bets with oneself when one goes to a place where there was once a statue or picture of him – will it still be there today?

It wasn't, of course. All that remained was a freshly white-washed wall.

We made our study plans individually with the supervisor to whom we had been allocated. Of the fourteen of us I can remember only three as having any serious academic goals. Brian Murphy was gathering material for a book on the use of aspects of the Russian verb. Aspects, often denoted by a prefix to the verb, can indicate to your listener how you did something as well as when you did it. They are among the most difficult areas of the Russian language for foreigners. It was a good choice of subject, as it meant that Brian could be hard at work while engaged in everyday conversation with Russians, whom he would suddenly pull up short to interrogate them on why they had used this or that aspect. The problem was that Russians instinctively get their aspects right; they can't usually explain why they have used one and not another. '*Ya propylesósila devyáty etázh* (I have cleaned the ninth floor with a vacuum cleaner)' announced our cleaning lady brightly, at which Brian pounced. Why <u>pro</u>pylesósila when she could have used a number of other prefixes? The unfortunate cleaner, assuming her skill with the vacuum cleaner rather than her aspectival usage was in question, indignantly defended her work. It would not have comforted her to know that some years later her remark was immortalised in Brian's book on the subject of Russian aspects.[5]

David Vere-Jones was a mathematician from New Zealand who had been persuaded by his Oxford professor to seize the opportunity of getting to know Russian achievements in his speciality, which to our amusement he called 'the theory of queuing'. He quickly won the Russians' respect by his mastery of his subject, and ours by his resourcefulness and determination in learning Russian, having known virtually none on arrival. The third was Roger Bartlett, who was fortunate to have the distinguished historian P. A. Zaionchkovskii as his supervisor, a man both solicitous and demanding towards his foreign post-graduate students.

The rest of us had cast around for subjects that would allow us an easy ride. I had assumed that my subject, *Soviet Criticism of Cervantes*, was abstruse enough for me to be left to my own devices. But my supervisor, Konstantin Valerianovich Tsurinov, turned out to be an expert. Had I hit it off with him I might have written at least an extended essay on my subject. But I didn't. He was known as a hard task master who made the girls cry, but also as a doughty supporter of favoured students. I was not to be among the latter. It was a struggle even to address him by his name and patronymic (pronounced at speed it sounded like K'sin V'yanich) as custom

---

[5] A. B. Murphy, *Aspectival Usage in Russian*, Oxford: Pergamon Press Ltd., p 21.

required, but more seriously I developed a strong physical aversion to this crabbed figure, cigarette always drooping from his lips. I took to agreeing to everything he said in order to finish our sessions as soon as possible and resist the strong temptation to push his face into his ashtray. Appeasement didn't work, however, as when I brought back an essay which blandly repeated everything I had read in the meantime he would interrupt his reading of it with barks of 'Statement of fact!' and 'Not scientific!' I did please him enormously by lending him my copy of a highly specialised bibliography of critical works on *Don Quixote* that I had acquired from New York through an American girl I had met in Florence. As our meetings became rarer and eventually lapsed altogether there may have been some sort of unspoken compact between Tsurinov and me: if I wanted my book back I would have to see him; he wouldn't make a fuss if I didn't, but he would keep the book. That is indeed what happened.

I did have a moment of panic at the very end of the academic year when I was called to a faculty meeting to give an account of how I had spent my year. I described rather feebly the few essays I had written for Tsurinov, who wasn't at the meeting. 'Did he approve of them?' asked the kindly professor Samarin. 'Not really,' I replied. 'Was he right to do so?' 'Well, yes, I suppose so ...' To my surprise a murmur of approval rose from the assembled academics. 'Ah, self-criticism!' enthused Samarin and promptly approved my report. Quite by chance I had observed the appropriate ritual of such meetings – criticism followed by self-criticism – and I was off the hook.

We were obliged to attend Russian languages classes in the clumsily named Faculty of the Russian Language for Non-Russians. For me they more than compensated for the barrenness of my core academic work. My class was run by the diminutive Irma Petrovna Slésareva. Somewhat bossy and ultra-sensitive to slights on the Soviet system ('Typical English malice!' she fulminated when one of our number wrote a snide essay on the Soviet one-party elections we had just witnessed) she was nonetheless one of those dedicated Soviet teachers who gave everything she had to her job. She drilled us in such difficult areas as Russian verbs of motion and the application of aspects to them; and she arranged for us to have a course in intonation, so that our Russian began to sound authentic. The language classes in Moscow filled many of the gaps left by my National Service nuts and bolts language and my Cambridge literary language.

Before my academic efforts finally collapsed I would read regularly in the Lenin Library. This was the USSR's principal library, originally the Rumyantsev Museum and in Soviet times renamed, like so many other institutions, after Lenin. It was conveniently placed in the centre of town, and the reading conditions for us foreigners – in Reading Room No.1, otherwise reserved for professors – were comfortable, if a little intimidating at first. Even more intimidating were the fearsome cloakroom attendants. I was often in trouble with my ingenious two-in-one overcoat. 'Together?' they asked in a puzzled way, seeing two coat tabs, indicating two coats to hang on their bank of hooks, but only me in front of them. I had to explain that it was really just one coat, so they hung it on just one tab. Unable to hold the weight of both coats, the tab would break. If the same thing happened to the other tab, my attempt to study was finished for the day: the cloakroom attendants refused to take a coat without tabs, and there were equally zealous janitors at the entrance to the reading rooms barring access to those who hadn't checked in their coats. It was Brian Murphy who solved the dilemma: 'Tell them a story involving your mother – they won't be able to resist that.' So one day, as I was about to be turned away, I described how my poor mother had selflessly given up her own fur coat to ensure her son didn't freeze in the depths of a Russian winter. Overcome with emotion, mothers and grandmothers all, the good ladies found a place to store my coat, and on my way out I even found the tabs sewn on again.

On 1st July 1962 the Library celebrated its 100th anniversary. *The Times Literary Supplement* asked the British Cultural Attaché in Moscow to commission an article on the subject from a regular British reader there, and the choice fell on me.[6] Re-reading the article, I am embarrassed to see how I avoided the ticklish question

---

[6] *The Lenin Library*, From a Special Correspondent, *The Times Literary Supplement*, Friday, 29 June 1962.

Moscow University: Enjoying the Thaw

of how the authorities controlled access to the Library's vast stocks so that ideologically harmful books were kept out of the reach of the ordinary reader and difficult to access even for the specialist. I might have asked my guides at the Library what they had done with the works of Stalin, now that he himself was rapidly becoming a non-person, but I was too polite to do so. Nor do I think that my interlocutors, mindful of their official position, would have found a way of discussing such a delicate issue without being thrown on the defensive and launching into a sterile ideological counter-attack. Above all, I didn't want to sour relations with the three librarians who manned the reception desk of Reading Room No.1, and to whom I was indebted for setting up the interviews on which my article was based.

The time I spent chatting to these librarians over the desk increased as enthusiasm for my studies declined. Nina, the senior librarian, in her late 30s, was a member of the Party, but she was not the sort of Party careerist I was to come across so often later in life. Dedicated, discreet and loyal to her friends, in England she would have been a pillar of her local church. Olga, a little younger, was adventurous – she had a Polish lover – and liked to scandalise us by referring to the 'all-seeing eye', meaning the KGB and its network of informers. Convention dictated that you didn't talk about these things.

The junior librarian was Lara, a dreamer in her mid-twenties, who when she finally summoned up the courage to talk to me, asked

On the Fringes of Europe

the question she always put to English people she met: was it really true that the standard of living was higher in England than in the Soviet Union? She was always hoping to hear that it wasn't, which might have reconciled her to her very humdrum existence in Moscow, but she never did. I don't know if she dreamt of me spiriting her away to a fairytale England, but we formed a chaste relationship, most of it conducted across the counter in the reading room. Lara had drifted into a loveless marriage, which naturally constrained our meetings outside the Library, but as spring and summer came we went for walks along the Lenin Hills below the great tower block where I lived. Lara had endured hunger during the

Lara

war and could name all the edible weeds, principally sorrel, over which we walked. Whenever her meagre salary ran out before the

Moscow University: Enjoying the Thaw

end of the month, she simply went without food for the remaining days. Her views on life and politics were equally basic. Like most Russians I met, she was unthinkingly anti-Semitic, and she absorbed unquestioningly the narrow patriotism she had been taught. 'Traitor!' was her comment on the defection of the ballet dancer Rudolf Nureyev in the summer of 1961. And, pointing to a young Swede at one of the reading room desks, she said: 'That man's a spy!' 'How do you know?' 'Because he's reading outside his declared subject!'

Music played a large part in my social life. Within a week of our arrival I was taking my place as second Flute in the 'Light Music Orchestra of the Humanitarian Faculties of Moscow State University'. Light music was not my *métier*, but as I was queuing to apply for the classical orchestra I was flattered to be snapped up by the light orchestra's conductor, who needed another flute player. I enjoyed the atmosphere and quickly made friends in the orchestra, some which lasted throughout my stay. But it soon became apparent that I couldn't cope with the difficult flute parts, all written out in manuscript. So I left within a month, knowing that whatever my fellow players may have thought of my skills on the flute, they would be far too kind-hearted to kick me out. In the meantime I had learnt something of life in the 'collective', as any organised group was called in the Soviet Union. Our first rehearsal was introduced by the secretary of the orchestra's Komsomol Committee with a speech on 'Lenin and Light Music'. It was apparent that nobody was taking in a word of it, but all affected to take the ritual seriously, and not even the bizarre appearance of an interloper, climbing tipsily in through one open window and out through another, was allowed to disturb the occasion. Like all amateur orchestras, we suffered from players not turning up to rehearsals, but the reason was peculiarly Soviet: students were being drafted out to farms in the Moscow region for a week at a time to help with the potato harvest. At the end of the first rehearsal I made a bee-line for the orchestra's very pretty pianist, Lena, and was able to walk her home in the warm autumn evening through the elegant streets of the old Arbat district. Like my room-mate Volodya, Lena marvelled at all the travelling I had done, but she didn't really marvel at me and kept her distance.

It was Mark, the orchestra's principal clarinet, who really latched on to me. He was a former army bandsman and fluent on the instrument, but his passion was philosophy. Within a couple of weeks I was pestering my long-suffering parents to order from our local bookshop some obscure works by Paul Tillich (1886-1965), a German-American existentialist Christian philosopher, who was Mark's special subject of study. Tillich purveyed an ideology that the Soviet regime saw as hostile, but his books, and many others I had sent out for me, including Bibles in Russian, all arrived safely, even though it was clear that they had been inspected en route – they were tied up in tell-tale Russian string. Ideologically suspect books were not officially banned in the Soviet Union, they were just impossible to find in bookshops. Tillich's works were kept in the 'closed stock' at the library, so Mark had to get numerous signatures every time he wanted to read them. I ordered the Bibles mainly for students who wanted to look up the many biblical references in the literature they were studying. Again, armed with the appropriate signatures, these students could consult a Bible in the Philosophical Faculty (Department of Atheism, of course), but having a Bible of their own saved them endless time. Mark's supervisor was green with envy at his student's haul, and it may have been to keep him 'on side' that Mark asked me to order a still more obscure book on Greek Philosophy for the supervisor. The giving and receiving of favours – known in Russian as *blat* – provided a more cohesive fabric for Soviet society than any ideological sense of purpose.

In many respects Mark was a model Soviet citizen. Like so many of his generation he had lost his father in the war with Germany. He was not politically active and told me he would never consider joining the Party, but he seldom voiced any criticism of the regime under which he lived, beyond chuckling at the absurdities it threw up. Like many of my acquaintances, however, under the veneer of conformity he needed to assert his individuality. He explained to me that the basis of his life was knowledge: he could feel self-sufficient when convinced that he knew things of which no one else was aware.

Mark was instantly recognisable as a Jew – by his features and by his name: Mark Samuilovich (son of Samuel) Kelner. There were

On the Fringes of Europe

many Jews in the cultural and intellectual life of Moscow, but anti-Semitism was never far below the surface and had been virtually official policy in the last years of Stalin's life, so the Jews were always wary of appearing to put their Jewish identity ahead of their Soviet one. When we had known each other for some time, Mark lent me a scribbled copy of two unpublished poems by prominent Soviet Jewish authors, Margarita Aliger and Ilya Ehrenburg, agonising over where their loyalties lay. I sensed a distinctive Jewish culture in Mark's home, where he lived quietly with his mother and brother. When I visited them, they were excited that a Yiddish theatre group was being allowed to perform in Moscow for the first time since the war, but it was given no publicity.

At home with Mark

Moscow University: Enjoying the Thaw

I sometimes thought that Mark was exploiting my friendship, especially when he put in yet another book request, or when we spent an entire morning struggling with his translation of Bertrand Russell into Russian – my poor understanding of philosophy competing with his weak grasp of English. But I was just part of his system of favours. In return he introduced me to a wide circle of his friends, including a professional acrobat and a pleasant couple from Leningrad who made me welcome when I visited the city early in 1962. Mark also took me to a lecture at the Philosophical Faculty by Professor A. J. Ayer, the doyen of British linguistic philosophers and natural heir of Bertrand Russell. In inviting Ayer the Russians had bitten off more than they could chew. He was not going to bend his opinions to suit his hosts and dismissed Marxist philosophers in the UK in half a sentence. He also dismissed his floundering interpreter from Intourist, the state tourist agency, saying he didn't want to engage in a 'music hall dialogue'. He handed the text of his speech to a volunteer from the audience, who tried to render it directly into Russian, with no greater success. In the question-and-answer session Ayer snapped, terrier-like, at the heels of the ponderous professors in the audience until one cried *pax!* by appealing to him to share his 'scholarly plans'. We all knew that to discuss one's 'scholarly plans' was to enter a cosy never-never land where nobody would be held to account.

On the Fringes of Europe

It was through music that I met the eminent American scholar, Harold Berman, the first foreign professor of law to spend an academic year in Soviet Russia. I once took notes on his behalf at a discussion among Soviet legal academics on the merits and demerits of jury trials, based on a viewing of the American film *Twelve Angry Men*. In the Cold War atmosphere of the time everything the 'other side' did was suspect: the Soviet regime regarded trial by jury as a bourgeois trick (through the selection of juries from among the propertied classes) while the West saw the Soviet practice of a judge with two lay assessors as little advance on the notorious three-man courts that dealt out summary justice in Stalin's time, so the subject was contentious. I recall the Soviet professors musing over whether I should be allowed to sit in on their discussion, but unfortunately I cannot remember anything about the actual arguments they deployed, which doubtless would have benefited from Professor Berman's presence. He lived with his wife and four children in a splendid apartment in the National Hotel, just down the road from my faculty, and I would drop in for tea. The Bermans immersed themselves in Soviet life as well as foreigners could and sent their younger children to Soviet schools. One of their daughters once burst in after school, dressed prettily in her regulation black dress and white pinafore, exclaiming excitedly: 'You've no idea how *bad* we Americans are!'

The musical contact was through the Bermans' son Steve, several years younger than me and a rather better guitar player. Not the seven-stringed Russian guitar, but the classical six-stringed guitar, which was alien to the Russians. Through Steve I soon found myself involved with the Moscow classical guitar community. It was one of those close-knit groups that were slightly suspect in the Soviet Union because they derived their cultural heritage from abroad (in this case 'Fascist' Spain). My Russian guitarist friends took their art correspondingly seriously. Nowhere in Moscow did I encounter the jolly, bumbling amateurism that I was used to in England, and my lack of skill embarrassed me. Worse still, once the central heating came on for the winter, my guitar was nearly ruined in the dry atmosphere of my room. It cracked, and the wood of the neck shrank so that the metal frets scratched my fingers. Desperate, I tried putting a damp towel on the radiator, but the stench it created brought the Sanitary Commission to my door with a threat to expel me. Happily, Steve Berman knew someone who could mend the guitar, and that in itself was an adventure. The picturesquely named Krivonos (Crooked Nose) had his basement workshop crammed to the ceiling with the remains of old upright pianos that he had picked up wherever he could. Not, he explained, because he played or made pianos, but because the wood from their backs was the best raw material he could get for making guitars.

Our British group found itself unexpectedly active as a male voice choir (we had left our two girls in Leningrad). It had started with our singing a couple of songs at the entertainment evening on

On the Fringes of Europe

Pictures at an Exhibition:

Some of our group at an exhibition of Soviet modern art, to which we had been invited by a Soviet youth magazine. We are looking deliberately glum so as not to appear to be appreciating 'socialist realism'

From the left: Bob Evans, his girlfriend Tanya, another Russian student, the author, Mike Schafer, Brian Murphy.

board the *Baltika*, when we found we had an accomplished choir master among us in the person of Barry Holland. He had perfect pitch and a good ability to communicate with us and with his audience. Flattered by our choir's instant fame in Moscow we accepted invitations to sing in schools and also at the *Dom Druzhby*, the House of Friendship. This was the headquarters of Soviet 'Friendship Societies' with foreign countries and the place whose canteen we used. We enjoyed good relations with the staff, but we were always wary of being exploited in the propaganda war. Some of us once stormed out of a concert we had been invited to when they began noisily to film us in the audience: we feared our pictures would appear in the entrance hall of the building among photographs showing foreign, mainly Third World, visitors eagerly lapping up Soviet culture. When our group was invited to sing at the *Dom Druzhby* we felt a compelling need to dissociate ourselves from the prevailing ideological atmosphere, and Barry with his usual aplomb introduced our closing number, *Old MacDonald Had a Farm*, as extolling a 'bright future for all mankind' (which was Soviet-speak for a Communist-dominated world) before we launched into our well-practised repertoire of moos and grunts. The *Dom Druzhby* people were upset, but we didn't lose our dining rights.

The choir's biggest ideological challenge came when Irma Petrovna, our teacher at the Russian Language Faculty, pressured us into taking part in a competitive 'Evening of Soviet Song'. We protested that we were not familiar with Soviet songs, but we didn't have the heart to offend our dedicated teacher and eventually found a song that we could sing without feeling that we were in some way buying into Soviet ideology. It was a rousing but innocuous piece entitled *I Love You, Life!* The prize, however, went to the massed Chinese choir for their rendering of *Lenin is with us!* At that time the Soviet Union and China were fighting for leadership of the world Communist movement, but their public polemic was still nuanced. The Chinese choice of song was therefore significant: the way it sounded in Russian (*Lenin s nami!*) could only be construed as implying 'Lenin is with *us*, not you!' Irma Petrovna was clearly troubled: 'You have to admit it, they're an organised lot,' she mused apprehensively.

I was an enthusiastic concert-goer. Tickets for the Moscow Conservatory and the Bolshoi Theatre for ballet or opera were hard to come by, but we foreign students could get them at a discount from the major hotels, which in the off-season didn't use up their allocation for tourists. The great Russian soloists of the day – the violinist David Oistrakh, the pianists Emil Gilels and Svyatoslav Richter, the cellist Mstislav Rostropovich – were frequent performers, sometimes playing a programme of three major concertos in one evening. Dmitri Shostakovich's compositions were being widely performed. On 20th January 1962 I found myself at the Conservatory listening to one of his long suppressed works. This was how I described the occasion to my parents:

> Shostakovich's Fourth Symphony is having its first performances this year although it was composed in 1935-6. It was never played then for obscure reasons, but most probably because it was not simple enough for the standards required at that time, and Shostakovich was probably scared that if it went on, his head would come off. Anyway, last night I spotted many big musical people in the audience including 2 Oistrakhs and the composer himself. The symphony was very noisy and I couldn't make

much of it until the last movement which was quite lyrical. I couldn't help being moved by it because I was sitting just three rows behind Shostakovich himself, who was on the other side of the central gangway and was going through agonies of emotion which left him absolutely paralysed by the end. This emotion was obviously not put on as it was so undignified – he looked like a schoolboy who's been called up to see the headmaster.

Shostakovich had withdrawn the symphony himself in 1936 after Stalin's hostile review of his opera *Lady Macbeth of Mtsensk*. Its first public performances at the end of 1961 and beginning of 1962 were a consequence of the 'thaw' in cultural affairs introduced by Khrushchev's denunciation of Stalin. But the occasion had no special billing; the programme note gave only a hint of the symphony's troubled history; and there was no lionising of Shostakovich. I bumped into him in the interval, all alone, nervously smoking a cigarette on the stairs of the concert hall. Caution was the order of the day, as everybody knew that the 'thaw' could easily be followed by a late frost, as indeed it was, even before Khrushchev was overthrown in 1964. Tikhon Khrennikov, the Secretary of the Soviet Composers' Union, who had criticised Prokofiev and Shostakovich for 'formalism' at the Composers' Congress of 1948, was still in office. Indeed, he had attended a concert of my Light Music Orchestra, where I had been introduced to him as a sort of

On the Fringes of Europe

collector's item. He took absolutely no notice of me, which irked me at the time, though rather less so in retrospect.

There was a strong bias in the Moscow concert repertoire towards the major classical symphonies and concertos, and I yearned for something more intimate and pre-classical. For this reason I was an ardent fan of the Moscow Chamber Orchestra under Rudolph Barshai, who later emigrated to Israel. With just 20 players, all except the cellists standing up, they played Vivaldi and Haydn in a way that cleared my head of the thick textures of Tchaikovsky.

The Soviet theatre was also afflicted by gigantism. Most of the Soviet plays I saw had unnecessarily large casts, over-elaborate scenery and sometimes a complete orchestra to play incidental music. Melodrama won out over dramatic tension. The reason was that theatres, like every other 'unit of production', had a quantitative plan to fill – man-hours on stage, number of sets to be constructed and so on – so it was imperative that as many of the established repertory company of each theatre were in employment as much of the time as possible. The Moscow Arts Theatre (MKhAT), however, was under a different constraint when it put on its productions of Chekhov. Like the D'Oyly Carte productions of Gilbert and Sullivan operettas in England, the MKhAT was committed to productions of Chekhov's own time, as I could tell from the photos that adorned the theatre. To begin with, these 'Chekhovian' productions captivated

Moscow University: Enjoying the Thaw

me, but when I re-discovered them, unaltered, decades later they seemed unbearably stale.

Two Soviet plays fired my enthusiasm, however. The first was Mayakovsky's *Bedbug*. This was the play we had put on at Crail as National Servicemen, and I was agog to see it done professionally. I was not disappointed. 'The Russian style of over-acting is very good for this kind of rather crude comedy,' I wrote to my parents, 'and the whole thing made about the best evening's entertainment I have had so far at the theatre.' Even better was *The Emperor's New Clothes*, by Yevgenii Shvarts, based on Hans Christian Andersen's famous story, with the fables of the *Princess and the Pea* and *The Swineherd* woven in. The satire had been written in 1934 as a dig at the emerging Nazi regime in Germany, so the Soviet critics laboured to persuade us, but anybody could see that it applied equally well, if not better, to the Soviet regime itself, so there was something tantalisingly subversive about it. All theatre-going Moscow wanted to see it, and I was lucky to get a ticket by having friends who knew friends. In Moscow, theatre-goers tended to buy more tickets than they could use on the night, and there was always an informal market at the entrance to the theatre. It was a civilised system, with tickets changing hands at face value (ticket touts were unknown), and you could judge the popularity of a play by how far in front of the theatre the hopefuls stationed themselves to ensure they would be the first to accost the ticket-bearing theatre-goer. On this occasion, the moment I stepped from the Metro on to the platform I

133

On the Fringes of Europe

was met with the question (politely in the negative) 'You wouldn't have a spare ticket, would you?' The show lived up to expectations. The whole thing was rather like an English pantomime, done with considerable skill and wit. The sweet taste of forbidden fruit had something to do with its immense popularity, but in a cultural world dominated by the earnest 'positive hero', even in his more sophisticated, post-Stalin guise, entertainment pure and simple was a rare and precious commodity.

Entertainment of another sort was on hand with the approach of the festive season. For the Russians this was primarily the anniversary of the Revolution of 1917, celebrated on 7th November. The official celebrations involved a military parade through Red Square, with the Soviet leadership taking the salute on top of the mausoleum from which Stalin had been removed unceremoniously just a few days earlier. I paid no attention to this event, which in later years would absorb me professionally. I would never have got to the centre of Moscow, which was closed off to all but ticket holders, and in any case the Russian friend with whom I had stood bemused on Red Square a few days previously had invited me to lunch at his flat in one of the new blocks near our University hostel. I had no idea how a Russian lunch party went and turned up bearing a tin of peaches bought at the British Embassy shop, thinking that my host and his wife would enjoy something that they could not easily get hold of themselves. The pained expression on their faces immediately told

Moscow University: Enjoying the Thaw

me that I had made a grievous mistake – alcohol and yet more alcohol was needed to fuel this lunch. I had also expected a sit-down meal, but we didn't have a formal meal: a collection of pies, salad, fish and mushrooms had been laid out on the table beforehand. We ate in short bursts after drinking a toast in vodka or Armenian brandy, then talked for half an hour before another toast and another burst of eating. I had arrived at one o'clock, and as the afternoon wore on I realised I had made another mistake in buying a ticket for a concert by Rostropovich that evening. But every time I tried to make a getaway one or another of the guests would buttonhole me to whisper some confidence or other – usually designed to show me that he was different from and superior to the other guests. It was nearing eight o'clock in the evening when I managed to tear myself away and struggle along to the Conservatory with no more than the last half hour of the concert remaining. The staff would have had every right to refuse me admittance, but they displayed the Russian woman's traditional tolerance for inebriated men and guided me to the upper circle, where I stood pretending that I was swaying with enthusiasm for the music and not for any other reason. Luckily some of my fellow English students were at the same concert and guided me home.

The following day was also a holiday, and to clear our heads, my fellow student Mike Berry and I decided to go for a walk. In those days the hostel and the new buildings around it were right on the edge of town, and in no time we found ourselves among ramshackle huts and houses, where we stumbled across an impromptu street party, which broke up and dispersed on seeing two foreigners – try as we might, we could not look inconspicuous. But one unkempt woman of uncertain age stood and faced us aggressively. 'Where are your documents? You have come to mock us. You have come to steal from us. You have come to spy on us. Show me your documents!' Slightly mollified by our proving our identity with one of the numerous passes we always carried with us, she transferred her antagonism to the Chinese and invited us into her house. It was little more than a shed with a small window, furnished with a wooden table, a bench and a large bed. Pieces of bacon fat, crusts of bread and an empty bottle stood on the table. It was only after getting accustomed to the murky light that I noticed the sheets on the bed. In an otherwise dirty and decrepit dwelling, the sheets were spotlessly clean; and not only that, they were edged with the most intricate and beautiful hand-woven embroidery. Our hostess was far too preoccupied to be able to tell us how she had come by such magnificent sheets, and was soon busy pointing out to us her proudest possession. This was a radio, high up in the corner of the room, in the position where once an icon might have hung, the source, evidently of her jumbled political running commentary. 'That's all I do,' she said, 'listen to the radio and play with my cat.' At this a cat dutifully appeared from under the bed and, with a little persuasion, sat up and begged like a dog. When our new acquaintance played with her cat, her rough manner dissolved and the hostility she had shown towards us and the world in general

Moscow University: Enjoying the Thaw

disappeared. Transformed as she was by the presence of the cat, she seemed to forget about us altogether, so we took the opportunity to slip out quietly. We were soon back in the anonymity of modern Moscow, unexpectedly refreshed by the raw humanity of our chance meetings that morning.

New Year celebrations in the hostel were lengthy, as there were students from Siberia and further east who insisted on seeing in the New Year according to their local time, which could be anything up to nine hours ahead of Moscow. By that time I had anyway had enough of the festive season, having in the meantime celebrated an English Christmas. This festival was of course ignored by the atheistic Soviet State, and even by Russian Orthodox believers, since they went by the old Julian calendar and celebrated Christmas on 6th January. But the British Embassy took it seriously enough to parcel us students out to staff members for Christmas lunch. For Brian Murphy and me it was in fact an 'anti-Christmas' lunch (steaks from Helsinki, where Embassy staff could order choice meat, instead of turkey) given by two bachelors whom I was to find myself working alongside a few years later, Anthony Loehnis and Michael Duncan. We were also invited to the Ambassador's Christmas dance and to a Boxing Day party, where some of us students put on a well received cabaret. I was happy enough to enjoy the congenial company of people of my own background, but generally looked down my nose at the closeted life led by the Embassy people, little imagining that exactly four years later I would be part of it.

On the Fringes of Europe

By Christmas time the relentless pressure of Moscow life was beginning to tell on our group. As well as the practical difficulties, there was an emotional strain imposed by the many Russian friends we were making. Paradoxical though it may seem, they trusted us – foreigners from the 'enemy camp' – more than each other. The explanation was simple. In the ideological closed circuit in which they lived they were expected to report to higher authority on each other's lapses. Such tale-telling could lead to what was politely called 'unpleasantness'. Getting to the point of actually trusting someone who was nominally your friend was a long and fraught business. The Russian students knew that we foreigners would not report their confidences to the Soviet authorities, so we were from the start more trustworthy. Initially it was flattering to be confided in, but we were soon drawn so deeply into the problems of our Russian friends that any attempt to wriggle out was interpreted as betrayal. One of our group became so over-wrought by shouldering the burdens of the Russians that he had something of a nervous breakdown and had to go home early. Towards Christmas I mulled this over at length with Barry Holland, whose imperturbability and detachment I liked. We were both fascinated by the Soviet Union and thought it likely that our future careers would in some way be linked with it (Barry was to become Head of the BBC Russian Service, while I spent most of my Foreign Office career analysing Soviet politics). But we agreed that we would need to keep a severe check on our emotional involvement with Russia. This became something like a vow on my part, and I observed it during the forty

Moscow University: Enjoying the Thaw

years of my professional interest in Russia. It probably cost me some exciting and rewarding experiences, but it preserved my sanity and, I hope, my objectivity.

In the meantime, the best way of reducing the pressure of Moscow life was to get away from the city. We had had little opportunity to travel in our first three months, but in the New Year we expanded our horizons considerably.

On the Fringes of Europe

Five

Moscow University 1962: 'Our Boundless Motherland'

G etting away from Moscow was not easy. No foreigner was allowed to stray outside a forty-kilometre radius without permission, which precluded many short trips to attractive places in the Moscow region. True, some of us occasionally ignored the rule. We could simply buy tickets for the local train on a busy Saturday morning. There were many Soviet citizens whose native language was not Russian, and we would be taken for visitors from one of the Baltic republics. I recall 'stealing' a refreshing springtime visit to Abramtsevo, not far outside the limit, which in the nineteenth century had been a cultural hub.

But to go further afield we had to travel as a group, which meant mobilising the bureaucracy of the University's Foreign Department. Mike Schafer, our official group leader, wore himself to a shred trying to persuade the department's deputy head, the elusive and uncooperative Valentin Sergeevich Nazarov, to fix up a visit to Vladimir and Suzdal' during the New Year holiday. Today these two historic cities, 200 kilometres north-east of Moscow (and in mediaeval Russia far more important than Moscow) are a standard item on the 'Golden Ring' tourist trail and can be 'done' on a day-trip. In 1962 they were an adventure. I had never before experienced the vast expanses of snow that disguise familiar features of the landscape. The high point was a one-and-a-half kilometre walk through the frozen landscape to the lonely and beautiful church of Pokróv na Nerlí. Only many years later, on a summer visit, did I realise that the tiny church was set at the confluence of two small rivers, making it even more attractive. True, trudging round in deep snow at a temperature of -17°C with a smart wind blowing sapped my enthusiasm for the church architecture we were supposed to be admiring. It was here that I became painfully aware of the lack of a fur collar to my otherwise efficient home-made overcoat.

We had of course seen onion-domed churches in Moscow, but here I was entranced by the whole complex: gaily painted dwelling houses with their complicated decorations over the door, round the eaves and windows, the whole impression of yesteryear being enhanced by the many horses and sledges, even the children in sledge prams. 'This was *Russia* rather than the *USSR*!' I enthused in my account of the trip to my parents.

Moscow University: 'Our Boundless Motherland'

In Vladimir

From the left: Bob Evans (posing as Lenin), John Gunn, our minder Valentin Nazarov, Roger Bartlett, Mike Schafer, Brian Murphy, Arthur Meyer, who later took over from Mike Schafer as group leader, and our local guide Irina, sensibly shod in her felt boots, as she was about to take us across the fields to the little church of Pokróv na Nerlí (below)

On the Fringes of Europe

A month later, four of our group managed to arrange a private visit to another of the 'Golden Ring' cities, Yaroslavl'. We went by bus for the sake of variety, a six-hour trip that more than sated my appetite for the Russian countryside under snow. It was beautiful when the sun shone, especially when there was hoar frost on the trees, but without the sun it became oppressively monotonous.

As with our previous trip, it was the glimpses of provincial life and the landscape that absorbed me far more than the historical monuments. Even though I was half-way through my time in the Soviet Union, I was still capable of being surprised by confrontations with Soviet life that did not fit the sanitised version we were fed by the press and radio. On this occasion it was a crowd of gypsy women, who surrounded us on our arrival in Yaroslavl'. I was incautious enough to give one the token sum of twenty kopecks. Pocketing this, she started telling my fortune in a language akin to Russian, but not near enough to be understandable. She then asked for a rouble, promising to give it back. She spat on it, made me spit on it, talked away, made me turn a mirror over in her hand and then demanded a note of higher value so she could tell my fortune further. By this time the bus driver, who had promised to give us a lift to the hotel, was getting impatient, so I kept my five rouble note, left the gypsy with the rouble and with great difficulty got away from her (she was clutching me with a fairly muscular grip), at which she promised me nine years of suffering for 'mocking us' – the only part of the fortune-telling I understood. In fact, though they concealed it well, the gypsies were obviously the ones doing the mocking. One of my travelling companions had to part with three roubles, no mean sum to us, before escaping the clutches of his gypsy.

Then there was the landscape, which was in fact more like a seascape. This was my first view of the legendary Volga – a relative slip of a river at this stage, but still about a quarter of a mile wide and frozen over completely except for a channel at the side where a factory discharged hot water. A bridge had been built to cross this point, leading on to an ice road across the river that could take any sort of traffic – an amazing sight to me, whose only previous experience of a river of these proportions was the River Plate in Argentina.

Yaroslavl': the ice road across the Volga

After a couple of days in Yaroslavl' we returned to Moscow by local buses via another 'Golden Ring' city, Rostov Veliky (meaning 'the Great'), at one time bigger than Yaroslavl' and with its own large Kremlin. But now it exuded the dreariness of a Russian provincial town. We had quite a good lunch in the only café there, but it had more than its fair share of drunks at midday, possibly because our visit, on 23rd February, coincided with the official Soviet Army Day. We also inspected the market, where people from the collective farms were allowed to sell spare produce, but evidently they hadn't any, as there was nothing and no one there except for two peasants selling milk and sunflower seeds. We were entering the worst time of the year for food: menus were getting shorter and queues longer. Rostov nonetheless yielded a treasure for one of our group – he bought eight table tennis balls, which couldn't be obtained for love or money in Moscow. Such were the vagaries of supply and demand in the planned economy.

Earlier in February 1962 we had done a group trip to the Baltic Republics and Leningrad. Vilnius, capital of Lithuania, was our first stop after 15 long hours on the train – 'hard' class at that. In the Soviet scale of things Vilnius was not that far from Moscow. I was constantly making a fool of myself among my Russian friends by sticking to a British scale of distances: they had laughed when I maintained that at Cambridge University I had to live in as a boarder because my London home was so far away – a good two and half hours by train. Two and a half *days* was their idea of far away. Nor had I any idea of the diversity of peoples and places within the Soviet Union. 'There are various gothic style buildings [in Vilnius] and the whole place is very un-Russian, which is a pleasant change,' I wrote excitedly to my parents. There was a familiar, European feel to Vilnius and Riga, the capital of Latvia. It would have applied even more to Tallinn, capital of Estonia, geographically and linguistically close to Finland, where the inhabitants could watch and understand Finnish television. To our disappointment, however, we had to miss Tallinn out: the town itself was 'open', but the route to it (unless we went back to Moscow and out again) 'closed' – a situation frustratingly familiar to foreign travellers in the Soviet Union.

Russians loved to travel to the Baltic coast – they called it 'our abroad'. Here they could pretend they were in Western Europe, itself inaccessible to all but the privileged few. The propaganda machine made much of the size and diversity of the Soviet Union itself – 'Our Boundless Motherland' – so as to convince the populace that they had no need to travel to the real abroad. For all that, the rouble, the ubiquitous Russian language, and the policemen's uniforms left you in no doubt that you were in the Soviet Union. Nor could you escape the Soviet propaganda campaign of the moment. At that time it was Khrushchev's panacea for the country's agricultural problems, the mass cultivation of sweet corn, even in the northerly Baltic region, to which it was hardly suited. 'Sweet corn again!' muttered a disgruntled visitor to the Exhibition of Economic Achievements in Vilnius, as he turned on his heel and walked out.

After six months cocooned in Moscow, and woefully ignorant of the brutal incorporation of the Baltic States into the Soviet Union in the war years, I was unprepared for the deep hostility towards Russia that we encountered among the native population of Vilnius and Riga. I recall in particular an elderly shop assistant. Not only was she unimpressed by my Russian, which was better than hers, but wanted to know why, as an Englishman, I should learn it at all when I didn't have to. And among the students we met, a devout Catholic told us in tears that she had been pressured into joining the Komsomol. Somewhat chastened, I was pleased to be of some use to our hosts – on this trip we were not holiday makers, but a 'delegation' – by spending some time recording English vowel sounds at a teachers' training college.

In Leningrad, again as a 'delegation', we were allowed to visit the tourist sites only after we had dutifully admired the local authorities' pride and joy, the Soviet Union's first 'Palace of Weddings'. The Bolsheviks had decried marriage as a bourgeois form of economic enslavement: the Soviet State had initially sanctioned nothing more than a utilitarian form of marriage registration. But elaborate wedding ceremonies were now being encouraged to enhance people's sense of well-being in the post-Stalin 'thaw'. Leningrad had equipped for this purpose one of the many fine palaces that used to belong to the nobility. It included a bride's room and a groom's room, together with a shop where you could buy presents and rings, as well as the actual registration room with what looked rather like an altar at one end. On it stood a bust of Lenin in benevolent rather than revolutionary mood, while appropriate music was piped from some unseen source. It was a conveyor belt system, nonetheless: there was time for two couples to be married in the presence of eleven sheepish Brits before we could escape.

We didn't see much of our fellow students from the UK in Leningrad, but we did stay in their hostel, which gave us an insight into the conditions in which they lived – hot water only two days a week and then only for four hours at a time, and pretty smelly sanitation. I still thought it would have been better than Moscow – the hostel was very near the university and the centre of the city, and it didn't have the monolithic, anthill atmosphere of the Moscow hostel. Captivated by Leningrad, I had got permission to stay on for a couple more days after the group returned. But I was thrown out of the hostel and had to find accommodation at the other end of the scale – a plush suite at the Astoria Hotel, where instead of being eleven to a room I seemed to have eleven rooms all to myself, at a correspondingly exorbitant price, or so it seemed to me as a student.

I managed a further private visit to Leningrad at the beginning of June in order to see the famous 'white nights'. The attraction is not just that the sun scarcely sets at that time of year, but that one side of the sky is quite dark and the other side light, with dusk and dawn merging into one, while the setting/rising sun picks out gold highlights on the city's domes and spires – a magical sight. On that occasion I had my fill of a white night when I found I had been locked out of my hostel and so was forced to wander around the city till six in the morning, admiring its beauty and lamenting its lack of all-night cafés.

Our group travel plans included a major trip at the end of the academic year in the southern regions of the Soviet Union, taking in the capital cities of Soviet Central Asia and the Caucasus. I was appalled at the intensity of the planned itinerary in the summer heat and put forward a counter-proposal to go to Siberia and have a quiet time fishing in Lake Baikal. Not surprisingly, my idea was rejected both by the authorities and my fellow students, but at least the Central Asian leg of the trip fell out of the plan. This was not as a result of my pleadings but because the Soviet Ministry of Higher Education, upset that the Soviet students in England were not being given a similar round trip at the end of the year, withdrew a substantial number of the roubles they had put up for our trip.

So on 19th June we flew to the capital of the Soviet Republic of Azerbaijan, Baku. It was suffused in a smell of oil, and for the first time I saw the small pumps called 'donkeys' drawing oil from under the shallow waters of the Caspian Sea. The sea itself was oily, and bathing not much fun. It did introduce us to Soviet beach manners, which were lackadaisical. Many people didn't have swimming costumes and just stripped off to their underwear to swim. They included our lady minder, who showed a remarkable lack of inhibition in letting her ample flesh spill out all over the place from her bra and knickers.

The Caucasus was full of reminders of Russia's imperial past. We arrived at our next stop, the Georgian capital Tbilisi, by way of the Georgian Military Highway, which in the nineteenth century had carried the Tsar's armies over the mountains to assert his empire's control over the region. Everything in Tbilisi evoked wine, including the Georgian alphabet, which looked like bunches of grapes in various arrangements. Stalin was Georgian, and I learnt enough of the alphabet to be able to pick out his mother's grave in a local churchyard to which we were directed. We were always on the lookout for interesting locals to talk to, but found few Azerbaijanis in Baku and few Georgians in Tbilisi: everyone seemed to be Armenian – they were spread widely across the two republics. The Armenians in turn felt squeezed by the Kurds, who occupied a sizeable part of Armenia. 'They're not like other humans,' confided one Armenian, 'they breed twice a year.' In 1915 the Armenians had suffered grievously at the hands of the neighbouring Turks during the upheavals of the First World War. The Soviet authorities suppressed the issue in the interests of good state relations with Turkey, but they could not expunge it from the Armenian consciousness. As our train trundled through the day alongside the border with Turkey, my Armenian neighbour drew my attention to a spectacular mountain in the distance:

- That's Mount Ararat, Armenia's holy mountain.
- But it's on the Turkish side of the border!
- *Poka!* (For the time being!)

Yerevan, Armenia's capital, seemed a rather bland Soviet city, but visits to Echmiadzin, the centre of the ancient Armenian Christian church, and to the huge, deep, blue and very cold Lake Sevan, up in the mountains, were more than rewarding.

From Yerevan we went by train to Sukhumi on the Black Sea coast. It was a prim and proper Russian seaside resort – a run-down Eastbourne. It was so prim that when three of us took a rest from our walk along the promenade by sitting on a low wall in front of a villa, we were given a ticking off by a passing Russian. 'We don't behave like that here,' he explained, pointing out that there were plenty of benches in the parks and along the sea front – they were the appropriate places to sit.

It was in Sukhumi that I first became dimly aware of the complexities of the Soviet federal system. We were still in Georgia, one of the fifteen ethnically based 'Soviet Socialist Republics' that made up the USSR, the Union of Soviet Socialist Republics. But some of the republics themselves contained substantial ethnic minorities. Georgia, a small but mountainous territory with many different ethnic groupings, contained three subdivisions: Sukhumi was the principal town of one of these subdivisions, the Abkhaz

Autonomous Soviet Socialist Republic. All this was done in the name of the Soviet 'nationalities policy' that gave ethnic minorities a certain status and served to obscure the fact that the Soviet Union covered almost exactly the same territory as the Tsarist Empire it had overthrown. The awkwardly shaped package held together well enough when the strings tying it up were firmly in the hands of the rigidly centralised Communist Party in Moscow, but when in the 1980s they began to fray and break, the package fell apart, and nowhere more violently and bloodily than in the Caucasus.

From Sukhumi we took the steamship *Pobeda* (*Victory*) to Odessa. It was not the idyllic Black Sea cruise we had imagined, since the upper decks of the ship were crammed with deck passengers, so there was nowhere for us to sit. Luckily we were only on board for two days, and the trip gave us a chance for a brief stop in the Soviet Union's prime seaside resort of Sochi. We had now left the Caucasian Republics and were back in Russia proper – the clumsily named Russian Soviet Federative Socialist Republic, by far the biggest of the republics. Sochi was the opulent playground of the Communist Party leadership, who had their official villas discreetly hidden in the luxuriant sub-tropical greenery. A holiday on the Black Sea was always an uneasy time for a Soviet leader, however, as absence from Moscow left the field open for rivals who remained in the capital. In 1964, two years after our trip, Khrushchev was deposed in a coup while on holiday in Sochi, and in 1991 Gorbachev suffered a similar fate, although only temporarily. Ordinary Soviet citizens could holiday in Sochi as well. They would get a voucher that allocated them a place in one of the many sanatoriums maintained by their factory or other place of work, which explained why there were hardly any hotels, restaurants or places of amusement along the sea front and why few families holidayed together: mother and father would get their separate vouchers, while their children were sent to a Pioneer camp or to grandparents in the countryside. Since most families lived in far too close contact with each other in their crowded communal flats, separation may have been less of a loss than it seems.

After Sochi we spent a few hours in the unappealing industrial port of Novorossiisk, swathed in a thick cloud of cement dust. We continued westwards past the tip of the Crimean peninsula – from the steamer we could see the villa in Yalta where in February 1945 the allied leaders had sketched out the post-war division of spheres of influence in Central Europe – until we reached Odessa, which I was excited about. A major port on the Black Sea, it had once been a cultural and ethnic melting pot. It was the scene of a revolt in the Tsar's navy in 1905 on a battleship named after the founder of the city, Count Potyomkin, Catherine the Great's favourite. The event had been immortalised in the 1925 film *Battleship Potemkin* by the Soviet director Sergei Eisenstein. Odessa had also featured as a vibrant city of the 1920s in the stories of Isaac Babel', to which Brian Murphy had introduced me. Babel' had been executed under Stalin, and his work was only just coming back into the public domain. But Odessa was a disappointment. True, we saw the famous steps down which the Tsar's soldiers advance in Eisenstein's film, shooting as they go, but the *Moldavanka*, where Babel's Jewish anti-heroes operated, was a staid and unremarkable Soviet street. Nor could I detect anything Ukrainian about Odessa: everyone spoke Russian, although by now we were in the Ukrainian Soviet Socialist Republic.

We were back in Moscow on 5th July 1962 after just over two weeks of travel. In addition to two Baltic republics, we had now travelled through four more of the Soviet Union's fifteen republics – exotic and colourful, but uniformly Soviet and to that extent not providing much of a sense of adventure. I could scarcely have imagined what would come to pass in this region a generation later. In 1988, when the Soviet Union was beginning to unravel, any of the Armenians we had met who were still living in Baku would have been expelled or killed in the blood-letting that was part of the struggle for control of Nagorny Karabakh, a mainly Armenian enclave inside Azerbaijan. The scenic railway line along the border with Turkey was closed as a result for much of the 1990s. In 1992, fighting between the Russian-supported Abkhaz and newly independent Georgia destroyed much of Sukhumi, including, doubtless, the little wall that we were impolite enough to sit on thirty years earlier. Today, simply to retrace the route of our summer trip would involve crossing the borders of five independent countries

On the Fringes of Europe

(Azerbaijan, Armenia, Georgia, Russia and Ukraine) as well as one (Abkhazia) recognised as independent by Russia but by no one else.

Against this background it is easy to understand how Russians of my generation and the next will have found nothing wrong with President Putin's outrageous claim in 2005 that the collapse of the USSR was one of the greatest geopolitical catastrophes of the century.

Brian Murphy and I had decided to leave for home earlier than the rest of the group. There was nothing more to be done in Moscow, and he had his family waiting, while I was more than ready to go back to my home comforts. We had just a day or so in Moscow after our return from the Caucasus to prepare for the journey home. It was a tense time. Brian and I had a last official hurdle to jump before we were free to leave. This was the dreaded OVIR – the Office of Visas and Registration. Only they could put the stamp on our passports that would allow us out of the Soviet Union. It was known that on instructions from the KGB they could bring up any past misdemeanours, real or not, and delay an applicant's departure.

Before that I had a difficult leave-taking with Lara. We had seen little of each other in recent months, not least because I had given up the Lenin Library the moment I had successfully accounted for myself at the Faculty. But Lara's fantasy required the relationship to have a tearful ending, and so we played it out. From the occasional

Moscow University: 'Our Boundless Motherland'

letter I received from Lara after my return I can see that I didn't play my part very well. I couldn't tell her that apart from rather having lost interest in our relationship my mind was elsewhere: I was worried stiff about Brian's and my impending visit to OVIR. Happily, there were no problems, and we took the overnight train to Leningrad, seen off by a crowd of Russian student friends. We were appropriately well oiled, and our taxi driver, sensing the occasion, pocketed the large rouble note I had proffered, saying: 'In the interests of Anglo-Soviet friendship, I'll keep the change!' We spent a day in Leningrad with my friends, then boarded another of the Baltic State Shipping Company's vessels, the *Mikhail Kalinin*, named after one of the few Soviet leaders who had managed to remain in office throughout Stalin's purges. We arrived in Tilbury on Saturday 14th July 1962. Brian's wife Joan and their three children were at the quayside. As we came down the gangplank their youngest, Dermot, gasped, 'Cor! Is that my Dad?' A year, albeit an academic one, is a long time in the life of a nine-year-old. My parents had rolled out the red carpet for me. Although my mother had her driving licence by that time, they had done what they always did on special occasions, hired a chauffeur-driven car from the Richmond firm of Grover's. And in those days a chauffeur looked like a chauffeur – peak cap and all.

It was a relief to get out of the Soviet Union. In those days one always talked about 'getting out' rather than 'leaving', such was the indefinable sense that the foreigner experienced of being caged in this vast and inward looking country. It took its toll on us: one of our Moscow group had to go home early with what appeared to be a nervous breakdown. And one of the Leningrad group took his own life that summer in mysterious circumstances that suggested he might have been subjected to blackmail by the KGB. But Russia is famous for exercising a hold on people once they have been there. Most of us went into careers connected in some way with the Soviet Union – academic, diplomatic, the press and broadcasting. Two married Soviet girls. We had been particularly fortunate in being able to enjoy a political 'thaw' that allowed us to mingle with ordinary Russians: a few years later students from the West were no longer allocated rooms next to Russians but were herded together in a single zone. For me the year in Moscow was a unique opportunity to gain some insights into the way ordinary Russians lived, and I drew on it throughout my career. Despite the stress it involved I knew in my bones that I would be returning to the Soviet Union and began to look around for work in that field. There were no immediate openings, however, and I jumped at the first job opportunity that came my way. In the early autumn of 1962 I was heading back east, but this time my destination was Finland.

Six

Finland 1962-1963:

An Affair of the Heart

In the summer of 1962 I visited the British Council to 'sign off' from Moscow and unexpectedly found myself 'signing on' to a teaching post in Finland. I had shown an interest in the idea of teaching English to foreigners and had indeed tried to get on a year-long British Council course in Leeds on the subject, but failed to do so as I was still in Moscow at interview time. My parents had rightly sensed that my efforts to join the Leeds course had more to do with prolonging my student life than preparing myself for a serious career, but the British Council called my bluff by offering me the Finnish post as a way of establishing whether teaching really was my *métier*. They had gathered their annual quota of some thirty teachers to scatter around Finland, but one slot, in the little town of Hamina, was still vacant. So I was fixed up for yet another academic year. I joined the rest of the teachers for a fortnight's course on how to teach English when you have no knowledge of the local language. It was run by Frank Billows, an engaging man who was well known in this field and demonstrated the art by teaching us some basic Turkish. '*Kitap*', he said, holding up a book, and then, putting it on the table, '*Kitap masada*'. He must have taught us something else during the fortnight, but that is what remained with me.

I didn't travel out with the rest of the teachers, as the Council had kindly agreed to let me first take a long-planned family holiday in the Lake District. So it was only at the end of September 1962 that I embarked once again on the Soviet steamship *Baltika*, just over a year since I had boarded it for my student year in Moscow. The trip had none of the previous year's excitement. It was the end of the season and there were only twenty nine passengers, one of them a sad alcoholic, on a ship that could take over four hundred. Nor did we stop at Rostock in East Germany, which I had been looking forward to re-visiting, because the *Baltika* was summoned to the rescue of another Soviet ship that had had an accident. The *Baltika*'s 'Entertainment Officer' – the same Yevgenii, as the previous year – further soured the atmosphere by bringing up the tragic death of one of our Leningrad students that I referred to in the previous chapter. 'Didn't he fall off a tall building in a drunken stupor?' he asked, probingly. I didn't respond to Yevgenii, whom by now I could recognise as a KGB officer. I was anxious to get shot of him and the murky world he represented, and as soon as we arrived in Helsinki on 2nd October I filled my nostrils with the refreshing, pine-scented air of Finland. As my bus trundled eastwards from Helsinki, I was enthralled by the landscape I was to get to know and love: the long, low line of dark green forest punctuated by huge granite boulders, remnants of the ice age, and by the delicate white trunks of birch trees, enlivened at this time of year by the flaming yellow of their autumn livery.

Not that Finland was far from the Soviet Union, with whom it shared its 1340-kilometre (838-mile) eastern border. Its whole history was inextricably intertwined with that of its 'big neighbour', as Finns would say with a wink that had something of a grimace about it. Finland had been ruled by the king of Sweden until 1809, when he had to cede it to the Russian Tsar at the Peace of Hamina – the very town for which I was heading. But Finland was never an integral part of the Russian Empire: it was a Grand Duchy; maintained its own legal and political system; and owed its allegiance to the person of the Tsar as Grand Duke of Finland, not as Emperor of Russia. It began to develop its own identity: the Finnish language gradually took its place alongside Swedish, while the imposition of Russian was stoutly resisted. So when the Tsar was overthrown in 1917, Finland was ready for independence. But the revolution in Russia fed into Finland's own deep social divisions: it was only after a short but bitter civil war that Finland established itself as independent not only of the Tsar's Russia but also of its Communist successor, the Soviet Union. Relations with that country continued uneasily until 1939, when Europe was moving towards war. Stalin decided Finland's border, within artillery range of Leningrad, was too close. Having failed to persuade the Finns to agree a new border, he invaded in November 1939. In what became known as the 'Winter War', the Finns, fighting for their lives on territory they knew well, put up a heroic defence against the ill-prepared Soviet forces. Although in March 1940 they were forced to sue for peace and cede the territory Stalin wanted, they maintained their independence and gained the grudging respect of the Russians.

That was not the end of the story. When Hitler attacked the Soviet Union in June 1941 he demanded from Finland the right of passage for his troops. Faced with the unenviable choice of another war with Russia or occupation by Germany, the Finns decided to fight alongside the Germans to regain their lost territories. In this 'Continuation War' they not only achieved this goal but pushed even further into the Soviet Union against the retreating Soviet forces. When the German advance turned into retreat, however, so did the Finnish, and in September 1944 Finland had to conclude an armistice with the Soviet Union on harsh terms: exhausted as they were, they now had to chase the remaining German troops out of Finland and embark on what looked like a crippling programme of reparations. Finland also had to promise never again to allow its territory to be used for an attack on the Soviet Union. This meant that in the Cold War that divided East and West from the late 1940s, Finland was not only debarred from joining any of the Western alliances, but even from giving the impression that it might be thinking that way. The credit for successfully pursuing this difficult policy was taken by Finland's long-serving president, Urho Kekkonen. He succeeded in winning the confidence of successive Soviet leaders, with whom he could hold his own in their favourite occupations of shooting, fishing and drinking. Under Kekkonen's leadership Finland persistently refused to pass judgement on the Soviet Union even after such blatant acts of aggression as the invasion of Hungary in 1956. As a result, Finland was sometimes equated in Western minds with the Soviet Union's Eastern European 'satellites', which had been occupied by Soviet troops after the war and forced to adopt the Soviet system. Finland was actually quite different. It had not been overrun by the Soviet Union. Helsinki was in fact one of only three capitals of European belligerent countries that had not been occupied at any point, London and Moscow being the other two. Despite the harsh terms of the peace agreement, Finland had once again succeeded in maintaining its independence, its own political system and its own way of life.

The Finns whom I met cherished their country's history. In many drawing rooms I would see a portrait of Marshal Mannerheim – their Churchill or de Gaulle – who had led the 'Whites' to victory over the 'Reds' in the civil war, who had commanded Finnish forces in the wars against the Soviet Union and who had been president for a short while after. In some drawing rooms I would see a large map of the Karelian Isthmus, a poignant reminder that the family had been evacuated from this lost territory, which would never be returned to Finland. In the nature of things I saw less of the still powerful left-wing movement in Finland that did not share all these sentiments, although I felt its effect – labour disputes and strikes seemed to be endemic. But the overriding impression was of an industrious nation working its way towards the high standard of living it was soon to enjoy. Paradoxically it was the Soviet Union's unprovoked attack in 1939 that had done most to unify the country and heal the divisions left by the civil war. Even the reparations regime had had a positive effect, forcing the Finns to branch out from their traditional industries based on forestry to such areas as specialised shipbuilding. Nokia was still making high quality rubber boots, but doubtless inventive minds there were already at work on the strategy that would turn it into one of the world's leading manufacturers of mobile phones.

Hamina was just 40 kilometres (25 miles) from the post-war Soviet border and had repeatedly changed hands in the various wars between Sweden and Russia in the eighteenth and nineteenth centuries. It was a fortress town, designed on an octagonal pattern, with its main arteries radiating from the Town Hall in the centre. Linking them were a 'Little Ring Road' and a 'Big Ring Road', and the whole town was surrounded by a rampart. Hamina boasted a military officers' school, which remains the town's best known

Finland: An Affair of the Heart

feature among Finns, many of whom have been based there at some time or other during their military service.

Hamina in 1962

My Rotary Club employers didn't introduce me to historic Hamina, being wholly immersed in the present day. The previous year's chairman, Baron Claes Cedercreutz, came from a Swedish-speaking noble family. The title had no significance in republican Finland, but the family was recognised to be at the top of Hamina society. The dynamic Cedercreutz didn't need to flaunt his title to earn respect: he was one of the country's leading surgeons. Intriguingly, his hobby was making jig-saw puzzles with a fretsaw. 'It's my way of relaxing after work,' he told me, 'I'm still cutting things up with my hands, but it doesn't matter if I make a mistake.' The current chairman was Jaakko Aalto, also Swedish-speaking despite his Finnish name. He ran a business in the harbour. Although Hamina's population was then just 10,000, it was Finland's third biggest port, and that, along with the garrison, was where the town's economic activity was based.

Finding me a room had been difficult. So as not to waste heat, the Finns have always built compactly, and few houses or flats would have a spare room. My predecessor had lodged with the Cedercreutz family, but their three children were growing up, and they must have reckoned they had done their bit. The Kaukonens, with whom I was eventually found lodging, were in a comparable situation with two teenage boys, a three-year-old girl and a dog, but for some reason had a large flat in a brand new block. It was in fact two flats put together, so not only did I have a room to myself, but my own front door as well. I enjoyed the comfort and admired the quality, style and ingenuity of the flat's design – this was the period when Finnish architecture and design was making a name for itself in the world. But my life there was quite solitary. Mrs Kaukonen was a nurse in the garrison hospital; her husband had been unable to find a job locally and was working in Helsinki. We had scarcely a word in common, but Mrs K and I eventually found ways of communicating, with her trying to anglicise her limited Swedish and me adding a few words of Finnish to my vocabulary every day. My best companions

Finland: An Affair of the Heart

Mrs Kaukonen in her nurse's uniform

were the little girl, Sirkka-Liisa, and the dog. Teaching myself Finnish was difficult – it was as complex as Russian, but had nothing in common with that language, or with any of the other languages I knew. Besides, I lacked incentive: my ignorance of Finnish was my strongest card as a teacher. Many of my pupils had a reasonable grounding in English, but were scared to open their mouths to speak it: with me they knew they had to.

My teaching programme was fairly light. There was no Finnish-British Society in Hamina, so unlike most of the other English teachers I was spared the task of running lecture programmes and social events. I undertook to teach 25 hours in the week under a system that had been running for a number of years, so those groups and individuals who booked themselves in for classes from year to year were already on my programme when I arrived. Others added themselves to it as time went on. It was very simple to arrange – they fixed a time with me and paid their fees to the Rotary Club, which in turn paid me a regular salary as well as providing me with free lodging. Most of my pupils were adults. A number worked in the harbour and needed some English to use with visiting crews. For others, the weekly English class was a hobby; they didn't demand much of me as a teacher, nor I of them as pupils. My predecessor in the job was something of a language buff like me, so I found myself initially teaching some Russian, French and Spanish to enterprising pupils. It was fun, as I had a far more structured knowledge of these languages than I had of my own. My knowledge of English literature and culture was also woefully inadequate, and I was at a loss for a subject when invited to give a talk to the Finnish-British Society in the neighbouring town of Lappeenranta. I settled on the topic that was gripping the world at the time: the Cuban missile crisis. In October 1962 the world had been on the brink of a nuclear war following a Soviet move to place missiles in Cuba – America's back yard – and so upset the strategic nuclear balance. I claimed in a letter home that my audience of a dozen or so were impressed by my talk, based entirely on my reading of *The Observer*. The British Council, to whom word of the unusual topic got back, was not, and ticked me off for straying well beyond my brief as a purveyor of English culture.

Finland: An Affair of the Heart

I did most of my teaching in the evenings, and my main concern was not my pupils' standard of English, but what they might offer me to eat. I was given luncheon vouchers to use at a local cafeteria run by an immigrant Italian, Giovanni (pronounced Kiovanni by the Finns, with the stress on the first syllable, as in Finnish words). He served a set lunch with a glass of milk, which in those days was standard in Finland. It kept me going well enough till about five o'clock, but at that point I started teaching till about nine, so I was dependent on my pupils for any further sustenance. They were mainly well off, from the middle to upper echelons of Hamina society. The mayor and his wife, who lived in a pleasant wooden house, would give me coffee and delicious cakes. The bank manager, who lived in an overheated modern flat, dispensed with the formal classroom structure altogether: we chatted in his sauna, after which his wife joined us for a meal.

After a while, several of the families whom I taught surprised me by saying, 'Come and have a bath with us.' I had known about the Finnish sauna, as I had known about the Russian *banya*, but before the bank manager had not had direct experience of either. Both are based on the principle of sweating the dirt out of the pores of the skin in the steamy atmosphere created by throwing water on hot stones. The Russians like to contrast the wet heat of their *banya* with the dry heat of the sauna, but to me the real difference is that the *banya* is communal and noisy, the sauna private and quiet. In the past it involved the cleansing of the soul as well as the body. The hero of Ingmar Bergman's film *Virgin Spring* has a sauna before he launches into the bloody slaughter of the robbers who have raped and murdered his daughter. Common sense and hygiene would have suggested doing it the other way round.

In rural Finland a century ago the family went for their sauna on Saturday evening to cleanse themselves in preparation for Sunday: however urgent the harvest, they would dress in their best clothes and do no work. The high jinks now associated with sauna, jumping in the lake or rolling in the snow, came in with the recreational sauna: in a traditional farming community you didn't build your house by a lake, which would have been thoroughly impractical. I boldly leapt into the water from a lakeside sauna in May 1963. The ice had scarcely melted off the surface, and I shot out again like a cork from a Champagne bottle. For a while afterwards I felt as if I had drunk the whole bottle as well and didn't repeat the experiment till high summer. Rolling in the snow was also an uncomfortable experience, which I felt had been oversold: the snow turned immediately to ice and stung me unpleasantly. Moreover, on the occasion when I tried this, my wet fingers stuck to the ice-cold metal door handle of the house when I tried to get back in to the sauna, nearly tearing the flesh off. Beating oneself with birch twigs, however, does belong to the tradition and is far from being the masochistic experience it might seem. The birch twigs (which must be in leaf) have a soothing effect on the skin and are credited with transmitting some healing process to it. How true all this is I don't

Finland: An Affair of the Heart

know, but I do know that when my parents came to visit Finland some four years later, they maintained that the sauna had cured all their aches, pains and warts, and promptly had one built in their Twickenham home.

I had three formal, classroom commitments. One day each week I enjoyed a pleasant outing to the nearby town of Inkeroinen, 40 minutes away by train, where I taught two classes at the big paper factory of Tampella. Later it swelled to a third, when a number of the factory's manual workers with no knowledge of English expressed an interest, and here I used Frank Billows' *kitap* technique for the first and only time. In Hamina itself I had a couple of classes at the local equivalent of the Workers' Educational Association,

'The book is on the table': teaching at the Tampella factory

though I have an uncomfortable recollection that the initially well-attended classes soon dwindled to almost nothing. And at the large local grammar school I took a conversation class of half a dozen girls.

It was after the first of these school classes that one of the teachers took me aside, marched me across a classroom and pointed out of the window to a block of flats opposite: 'That's where we'll have our teachers' conversation class,' she announced. The group of teachers varied in size, but there were three core members. The first was the owner of the flat in question, the forceful Ulla Reinikainen, the junior teacher of Swedish and divorced mother of three. Then there was Matti Vilén, small (because of a spinal deformity) and acerbic, who absorbed English spy novels at great speed. He didn't actually teach at the school but his wife Riitta was the accountant. The third was the teacher who had taken me aside at the school, Raili Laaksonen, the senior teacher of Swedish, who laughed at my jokes even more than my sister Caroline and continued to do so even after she became my wife. This was an uninhibited group, whose English was good enough for us to engage in the sort of spirited repartee that was virtually impossible with most of my pupils, who lacked fluency and, above all, confidence. But I did do some serious work trying to eliminate the Swedish idioms from their English. They became the centre of my social life as well: we would also meet at Matti's house, where I enjoyed practising my elementary

Finland: An Affair of the Heart

Conversation class.
Clockwise from the top: Matti Vilén, his wife Riitta, another teacher who occasionally joined our class, Ulla Reinikainen, the author, Raili Laaksonen with a patch on her left arm covering the smallpox vaccination she had been given before going to Leningrad

Finnish on his two little boys, or at Raili's flat in Rauhankatu – Peace Street, so named as it was built on the site where the 1809 Treaty of Hamina had been signed, though this completely escaped me at the time.

Raili and I would have laughed at the idea that within two years we would be married, and we did laugh when by the end of my stint in Finland most of Hamina had long since paired us off. But we enjoyed each other's company. Raili was not particularly happy in Hamina. She had a language degree from Helsinki University and had gained her teacher's qualification at a Helsinki school. She had been working for a pittance at the Finnish Encyclopaedia and enjoying a varied social life in Helsinki when her father gently hinted that it was time he saw a return on the money he had invested in her further education, so two years before we met she had moved unwillingly to Hamina. Her fiancé had broken off their two-year engagement in 1959, so she was quite despondent at times. She was also giving lodging during term time to her thirteen-year-old cousin, Marjatta Jokinen, and seeing her through school. Marjatta's divorced mother had died tragically just over a year earlier, and Raili's parents had taken her in. For my part I was happy enough in Hamina, but lacked company, especially at the weekends. So I enjoyed Raili's conversation (English came easily to her, though it was fourth in line after Finnish, Swedish and German), her spaghetti Bolognese, her gramophone records and her wine. Alcohol was a rare luxury in the Finland of those years. Retail sales were a state monopoly: you had to be officially registered as a drinker before you could buy. Raili was reluctant to take this step – it sounded like admitting to alcoholism – but Ulla Reinikainen had no such inhibitions, so Raili bought her wine off Ulla, and *Côtes du Rhône Villages* became 'our drink'. When Raili returned from a visit to Leningrad with a record of David Oistrakh playing Shostakovich's first violin concerto, that piece became 'our tune'. I paid no attention to Marjatta. Apart from my not knowing how to deal with a girl of that age, we had no language in common. None of us knew at that time what a significant role she would come to play in our lives.

Finland: An Affair of the Heart

I had arrived in Finland with my head full of the previous year's experiences in Moscow and was much readier to talk about Russia than England, but I soon learnt that the Finns were simply not interested. I would make a lame joke about Hamina, with its radial roads, having been built on the same pattern as Moscow, but it always fell flat. So I had to savour the similarities and differences on my own. The contrasts could not have been greater. In Moscow, to get from anywhere to anywhere took ages and frayed the nerves. In Hamina I could walk from one end of the town to the other in twenty minutes. That was my first luxury. My second was that arrangements made with Finns seldom needed to be renegotiated, unlike in Russia. I suppose I used a telephone occasionally, but I don't remember doing so. I met people, fixed up our next meeting, and that was it. There was a quiet orderliness about Finland which came as a welcome contrast to the noisy disorder of Russia. In my rather lazy mornings before the teaching round started, I would stare out of my flat at the unchanging work routine in front of me. A small train would bring a load of logs from the harbour and deposit them in the yard under my window. A solitary worker would cut them into smaller logs with a chain saw and load them into a lorry, which appeared at regular intervals. At equally regular intervals the worker would disappear into a hut for a cup of coffee (presumably) before re-emerging to continue his monotonous work. Even disorder was orderly. Once I was idly looking at the empty scene (it was Sunday) when a police van drove up, a posse of policemen opened the door of the hut, and half a dozen paralytically drunk Finns fell out. The police quietly picked them up, deposited them in the van and drove off. There had been no remonstrations, and scarcely a word had been spoken, a scene unimaginable in Russia, despite the two people's common fondness for alcohol.

As winter closed in, Hamina began to look less attractive. The one public holiday before Christmas – Independence Day on 6th December – was to my eyes a sorry affair. We foregathered in the sleet to watch the military parade, and I scoffed at the slovenly way the soldiers shuffled through the slush on the market square. I shouldn't have done so. A month or so later, when I was out skiing on my own in the forest, I was startled by a platoon of soldiers on skis and in white camouflage. They appeared from nowhere and swept silently by, the last of the group pausing to light his pipe before nonchalantly speeding off to join the others. It was the ability of the Finns to move swiftly and silently through the forest – not their parade ground drill – that had struck terror into the hearts of Soviet soldiers in the Winter War. But in December there was still not snow enough to ski. Looking out of the window all morning became depressing. I went down with flu, and to pick my spirits up I decided to spend Christmas at home. I had, after all, missed the previous Christmas through being in Moscow, and although at the age of twenty five I was seriously trying to grow up and live independently of my family, I naturally gravitated towards home at Christmas time.

Finland: An Affair of the Heart

Raili enjoys the snow

When I returned to Hamina in January, the atmosphere of the place had been transformed. A sparkling carpet of new snow illuminated the landscape even in the long hours of darkness, and was dazzling in the ever lengthening days of bright sunshine. The long, cold winter of 1962-1963 was a misery for my family in England, but a delight for me. Hamina society picked up with the main event of the year – the Rotary Club ball. Never one for dancing, I had made up my mind not to go. 'But you must come,' cooed Mrs Cedercreutz, 'the *crème de la crème* of Hamina will be there!' It was not her blandishments, however, but a subtle piece of blackmail that forced me to change my mind: their seventeen-year old daughter was to sing a song at the ball. If she went as my guest she would be allowed to stay on – otherwise she would have to go home after her song.

She was in fact quite fun, and taught me how to do the fashionable twist: 'With your hands up, you pretend you are rubbing your bottom with a towel, and with your right foot you are putting out a cigarette.' Nor did the Cedercreutz family pay much attention to my protestations that in my ordinary lounge suit I would be under-dressed. I didn't realise just how under-dressed till I saw all the men in white tie and tails. I later learnt that the Finns tend to miss out the black tie stage in their gradations of dress. Forewarned, my successor in Hamina, a Scot, trumped them all by wearing the kilt.

Shortly after the ball I had to find new lodgings. Mrs Kaukonen and her family were moving to Helsinki, so someone else had to take me in. It was embarrassingly clear that there were no takers, so eventually the current Rotary Club Chairman, Jaakko Aalto and his wife Inge turned their unfortunate son out of his room and gave it to me. They lived very centrally, overlooking Giovanni's café, and with them I was less isolated than at the Kaukonens'. In fact I was in danger of a slow death from joining the family's hedonistic indulgence in unlimited coffee, cake and American films on television, which we viewed through a haze of Swedish and Finnish subtitles – under the law, both had to be given equal prominence.

The snow rescued me. The Rotary Club traditionally gave each visiting teacher a pair of skis. I had been looking forward to the day when I could use mine. True, my first attempt was a minor disaster, as I had made the mistake of storing my wooden skis in the overheated flat rather than outside on the balcony. They had dried out, and one of them snapped as soon as it met its first obstacle. These simple pieces of equipment were not expensive, however, and I was soon putting on my new pair and skiing straight off from the back door to spend my mornings exploring the woods and fields around Hamina, even skiing across the frozen bay for a lunch one Saturday. I finally dispensed with my ingrained notion that downhill was the only 'proper' form of skiing and that cross-country skiing was just 'walking on skis', as it appeared to the uninitiated. I had more 'white knuckle' moments meeting a dip and a bend on a narrow forest path, with no means of braking, than I had had on the steep mountainside in Italy, when I could always brake by turning sideways. It took the grammar school's annual ski outing for me to learn that my skiing was highly inefficient. 'You're just running on your skis,' said Raili and taught me to let the skis do their bit of the work by gliding as they were meant to.

That lesson was important, as during the Easter break in April I joined a group of Helsinki students and British teachers on a skiing holiday in Lapland. We travelled by overnight train to the point where Finland meets Sweden at the top of the Gulf of Bothnia and enjoyed a brief excursion to the Swedish side of the border. In those days Swedes still drove on the left hand side of the road, and we admired the clever road junction where you started in Finland on the right side and ended in Sweden on the left, without really understanding how you had managed it. We continued by bus to the little town of Äkäslompolo, where we were lodged in two big dormitories and given copious quantities of wholesome food at the beginning and end of each skiing day. To my surprise, Lapland was too warm rather than too cold, with temperatures above freezing during the day. The slushy snow was less enticing than the powdery texture I had become used to during the cold winter in Hamina. But Lapland had the attraction of the undulating *tunturi* (somewhat similar to a fell in the English Lake District), and once we got high enough the snow was skiable and the vistas breathtaking. To get there we had to make long ascents (no ski lifts in those days), but they were followed by quick and undemanding descents. I recorded in a letter home that I had taken one and a half hours to get up the *tunturi* and four and a half minutes to get down again.

By the time of my return towards the end of April, spring had arrived in Hamina. The days were lengthening quickly as the near total darkness that had preceded my Christmas visit to England gave way to the near total daylight that would accompany me home at the end of May. I was able to sunbathe on the warm rocks while contemplating the still frozen sea. Raili and I exchanged our skis for bicycles – an experience I found equally scary at first. Like their skis, Finnish bicycles apparently had no brakes, and there again I experienced a few white knuckle moments before learning to press back on the pedals in order to slow down (the drum brake being housed in the rear wheel). There was little time, however, to enjoy the delights of the approaching summer. The Finnish educational year came to an end promptly on 31st May so the Finns could make the best of their brief summer. My work was therefore also at an end and I was soon on my way home, again aboard the *Mikhail Kalinin*.

In Helsinki I had picked up a copy of Alexander Solzhenitsyn's recently published ground-breaking novel of prison camp life in Stalin's Russia, *One Day in the Life of Ivan Denisovich*, and was engrossed in it throughout the journey. Enjoyable as my year in Finland had been, I knew by then that teaching was not my *métier* and that I wanted to make my career studying the Soviet Union. Early in 1963 I had seen in *The Observer* an advertisement placed by the Foreign Office Research Department. They had a vacancy for a researcher in Soviet affairs and required precisely what I had to offer: a good knowledge of Russian and some knowledge of the Soviet Union. I applied enthusiastically, but baulked at the idea of spending most of my savings on a trip to London for the interview in April, so I passed up that opportunity, not realising how rare such openings were. I was thrown back on teaching again and found a summer job with Davis's School of English in Kensington. Determined to grow up at last, I left home and joined a group of young men I had known at Cambridge in a flat in Earls Court.

My immediate concern, however, was a visit by Raili. She had long planned to come to England, where she had been once before in 1955 as a summer help to an émigré Latvian family in Doncaster. She wanted to see them again, but also to see a bit of England

On the Fringes of Europe

beyond Doncaster. I offered her the hospitality of my parents' home. In April I had written to them:

I think a Finnish friend of mine will be coming to England on a visit this summer, most probably in June. If she does come, could we put her up? She's a very charming person and extremely easy to get on with, speaks excellent English. Just for the record, she's not my fiancée, nor likely to become so! Her name's Raili, pronounced like the Irish wing three-quarter.

The 'fiancée' sentence was later played back to me with a chuckle by my mother, but it was true at the time. Hosting Raili was simply a practical business, bedevilled by the fact that none of us knew quite when or where she would arrive. She was travelling on a cargo boat from Helsinki, in those days a pleasant and cheap option, but one that didn't sit easily with the precise schedule of the Nicholson family. She eventually turned up at Euston Station (having travelled down by train from Ellesmere Port in Cheshire) on the very Saturday when I was booked into a St Catharine's College dinner in Cambridge. My father, who was also going to the dinner, took himself to Cambridge by train, leaving me with the family car to meet Raili and bring her up to Cambridge, since there wasn't time to take her to Twickenham. There was scarcely time to get to Cambridge either: Raili insisted on first having her hair done at a

Finland: An Affair of the Heart

hairdresser's in Euston Station. Then, to add to my anxiety, somewhere along the road to Cambridge the motor of the Morris Minor Estate cut out, and the car glided to a halt. Flummoxed, I did what I had seen other people do in such circumstances, namely lift up the bonnet and peer inside. I could see nothing unusual, except that the oil cap had worked loose. So I screwed it on again and, more in hope than expectation, re-started the car. It sprang into life – and with that my relationship with Raili changed. No longer was I the pink-faced schoolboy she had known in Hamina, but an expert mechanic and an authoritative figure on my own territory. My male authority was confirmed in a less appealing way when Raili (whose country was the first to give women the vote) found on our arrival in Cambridge that while my father, my elder brother Robin and I were going to the College dinner, the ladies were excluded. My sister-in-law Mary kindly put Raili up for the night and had the brilliant idea of showing her family photos, so when Raili eventually arrived at our home in Twickenham she was well briefed and was soon at home in the welcoming atmosphere of Warwick Lodge.

Raili saw more of my family than of me, as by that time I was working at the Davis's School, but when the time came for her to leave on another cargo boat our relationship was quite different. Shortly after she left I sat down and wrote a letter proposing marriage. I think I understood what a momentous decision I was making, but felt no qualms about making it, and I didn't hesitate before slipping the letter into one of the red pillar boxes near my

Earls Court flat. Once I had done so, however, I was impatient for a reply. This was absurd, as Raili was on the high seas, and it was only some two weeks later that she and the letter were united. When they were, she sent me a telegram, sensibly asking for a grace period while she went home, thought it over and talked about it with her father. It was a much bigger step for her than for me, as it meant giving up a well-paid and well-respected job, as well as seeing her parents bereft of their only child. In today's world she could well have suggested that I come to join her in Finland, drifting and jobless as I was, but in those days the idea would have been outlandish, and it didn't occur to either of us.

At that point in the middle of 1963 my student days had come to an end. I had long known that my main aim in life was to find a wife, a home and a steady job to support both. I now had the promise of the first, but I needed the other two to make it a reality. A new chapter in my life was about to be opened. Private life would be dominated by home and family, working life by the arcane art of Kremlinology.

Finland: An Affair of the Heart

Engaged:
this photograph was taken at my parents' home in Twickenham in December 1963,
when Raili came for Christmas and our engagement was announced

On the Fringes of Europe

MAP 1: THE BRITISH ISLES

MAP 2: THE IBERIAN PENINSULA

MAP 3: FINLAND AND THE USSR IN EUROPE

www.ingramcontent.com/pod-product-compliance
Lightning Source LLC
Chambersburg PA
CBHW071501040426
42444CB00008B/1434